The Rise of

COMIC BOOK MOVIES

From the Pages to the Big Screen

Benny Potter, Dan Rumbles, and Jason Keen

Foreword by Chris Stuckmann

Published by Mango Media Inc.

Front and Back Cover, Interior Design, Theme and Layout: Roberto Núñez

Illustrations: Elina Diaz

ISBN 978-1-63353-343-1

"Please don't make the super suit green... or animated!"

Deadpool

CONTENTS

FOREWORD

I must've been three years old when my father brought
home that damned inflatable Batman. That godforsaken
sack of grey and blue plastic. I'm sure my father meant well.
I mean, I *was* a boy, and that *was* Batman. It made sense! My
memory of receiving the toy is faint, but what he did with it
later is as crystal clear as if it happened yesterday. You see, I
was a mischievous little one, and I just couldn't live without
perusing my father's cabinet of cassette tapes. It didn't matter
how great the band was—Creedence Clearwater Revival,
Dire Straits, The Beatles—if that shiny brown tape could be
removed, I was going to make sure my parents found me with
it all of its inside contents strewn across the entire room.

I don't blame my father for what he did, if I found *my* child
destroying my film collection, I certainly wouldn't react calmly.
But still, the image of that inflatable Batman *COMING ALIVE* is
burned into my brain.

Of course, it didn't really come to life. But at that age, I was
positive that when I crawled over to my father's cabinet,
opened it, and Batman popped out... I was witnessing the
demonic possession of an inflatable superhero.

My devious father had realized that the most effective way to
keep me from getting into his cabinet would be to terrify me.
So, he'd placed that horrible toy inside the cabinet, closing the
doors in just the right way so that when I opened them—and
he somehow knew I would—Batman would pop out. I cried for
a long time, and I've spent the last twenty-four years since
then hearing my father tell everyone with a pair of ears how
hilarious that was. Thanks, Dad.

But really, thank you, Dad. Because despite being scared to death of Batman for a few weeks, I eventually grew to love the Caped Crusader. I have no clue if it's because of that inflatable toy, but that is definitely my earliest and most impactful memory involving a comic book character.

Cut to a few years later, and I'm *obsessed* with the Christopher Reeve *Superman* movies, even the third and fourth one. I'd often imitate a drunken Richard Pryor, fumbling to hack into a computer: *"Both keys at the same time? Oh ho!"* I can recall Nuclear Man's silver fingernails scaring me. Don't ask me why. Those things were horrifying. My parents still tell people about how I used to run around the house with my underwear on *outside* my pants, and a bath towel tied around my neck. As far as I was concerned, I *was* Superman, dammit.

Soon, I became aware of *The Incredible Hulk* starring Bill Bixby, and tore through the house, flexing my boney arms like Lou Ferrigno. I crawled face-first down the steps like Nicholas Hammond in *The Amazing Spider-Man*, and instructed my sisters in the proper way to beatbox the show's funky 70's bass-line.

 "Stop laughing!" I commanded my family while watching Adam West in the satirical *Batman*. As a five year-old, I was convinced that program was high art. But when Michael Keaton came on the scene, I pretty much lost it. From then on, Batman was officially my life. *Batman Returns* was always my favorite. I loved Michelle Pfieffer as Catwoman, for reasons I probably didn't yet understand. I'm sure it had absolutely nothing to do with the scene in which she gave herself a "bath." Nothing at all...8 Superheroes have played a large role in my life, and not just for entertainment. I grew out of my shell thanks to those movies. It gave me something to talk about with classmates, and while most kids in the 90's were afraid to admit they liked "nerdy" things like comic books, I made some of the best connections in my life due to talking about those characters.

Still, as recent as yesterday—as of this writing—I perused my neighborhood comics shop, JC Comics and Cards, and talked with the owner. This guy has literally watched me grow up. Whether it is manga, anime, or comics, he can get it for you. Best comic shop in Ohio as far as I'm concerned. We've gone from chatting about *Dragon Ball Z* to in-depth conversations about how much we loved *Deadpool* and *Guardians of the Galaxy*.

Today, I understand that Adam West was going for a laugh when he couldn't get rid of that bomb, that Spider-Man being accompanied by a 70's bass guitar is hilarious, and to top it all off, I wear my underwear correctly. But that's not to say I'm never tempted to stretch those babies over my pants.

– Chris Stuckmann, Author and YouTube Film Critic

MASHING COMICS WITH HISTORY

 **BENNY**

When I was first asked to write a book, I was a bit taken aback. I'm a guy who takes comic books, condenses them down and adds in some music and flair for a dramatic recap of that comic. This was completely out of my wheelhouse, and I was a floored that I would get the offer. But then when they asked me to write about comic book movies, it made more sense. This is what I do: talk about comic books and the movies related to them.

Originally, the plan was to discuss comic book movies in the context of how we got from the worst to the best. But as I did the research and dived into these movies I discovered, that isn't how it happened. Everyone loves to think about those little gems that get mentioned but that no one has ever seen. Things like the *Nick Fury* television movie starring David Hasselhoff or the original *Fantastic Four* movie that was never actually released.

We all have fond memories of the bat nipples from *Batman and Robin* and memories of Christopher Reeve from *Superman*. But it's a jumbled mess in which timelines and ideas are mixed up. It's been so long, and so much has happened, that people just don't remember things properly anymore. I for one am guilty of that.

Now a recurring theme you'll begin to see with movies post-2005, after the era of the Spider-Man films and the Batman movie people wanted, is a larger acceptance for the superhero genre. The fantastic worlds of superheroes had become more acceptable largely due to a 10 shifted focus of the general public. For whatever the reason, people began to praise nerdy and geeky topics. Comic books directly benefited from this. Since the source material benefited, so did the superhero movie genre. We were hot on the tails of things like *Harry Potter* being a successful franchise and not just a single movie. Shows like *Lost* were doing well on television and showing that the general viewing public was looking for something with a deeper meaning, even if *Lost* never provided that meaning.

Addding to this acceptance, the world view had shifted. When I was a child, I was told I needed to throw away my childish things around eighteen and grow up. My parents used to teach me that I was supposed to go to college, get a good paying job, find a wife, have many children and that was life. This was a mentality instilled in them from their parents and their parents before them.

As the world shifted from having to hunt and kill for our own food, the human civilization has been constantly looking for purpose and what is normal. But as we crossed through the nineties, the world began to shift to become more about convenience. With convenience comes more free time to enjoy your life. When I was young, you weren't supposed to be reading comic books or enjoying fantastic worlds. You were a nerd or a geek if you did, and you needed to get your head out of the clouds and get a real job. But with the world becoming about enjoying your time, popularity in such topics has grown.

Instead of remembering *Batman* as something you read as a child, now you can go buy the newest comic. Instead of missing out on the latest movie because you have to stay late in the office, you can go see it and take calls on your smartphone if needed. What I'm getting at is this is where the acceptance came from.

These worlds that many of us have been in since we were children have become acceptable not because they got cooler, but because people actually have the time to enjoy them. So what we hope to accomplish with this book is to explain what happened with the superhero genre. Because a lot of the first movies were incredible and were listed as some of the best movies of all time. But eventually, superhero movies fell into a gutter of trying to sell topical ideas and toys.

That should have been the end of many superhero series, but a lot of companies realized they can try again. We'll be looking at some key franchises and how they rose, fell, and rose again. The fact taht they can rubber band back so easily has created a weird situation for the superhero genre in which companies are repeatedly making similar movies until the movie-going public enjoys one of them. But I can't argue with success, and we have now gone from a successful movie to superhero movies ranking among the highest grossing films of all time, elevating these superheroes and the fans of comic books.

We as geeks and nerds have gone from the outcast to the cool individuals who know all the fun facts you'll never get in a movie. Now our goal is to educate you about what has happened with each of these movies, and then to present the opinions and reviews of these movies from a nostalgic old comic book reader and a comic book reader that jumped on board in the recent years with the new material. You will also notice entire segments for Superman and Batman while Marvel is lumped together.

This is not due to some *fanboyism* or preference for DC over Marvel. It's actually based on the fact Superman and Batman have completely separate franchises, while Marvel is touted as a complete franchise to itself. Superman and Batman were handled separate from each other, but both learned from Marvel's successes and that is proven by the last film in each of their franchises. As this is such a very opinion-based book, I thought it would be fun to bring in the members of Comicstorian team and explain who each of us is.

I am Benny, and I run the YouTube channel Comicstorian. On a frequent basis, we take comic book plots lines, cut them up into a ten-minute video, and read back what happened in a dramatic manner. The goal is to give people a general idea of a story that involves their favorite superheroes and entice them to go pick up a similar book or the book we read itself to get the full story.

I have held discussions about superhero theory, lore and plotlines. I have been reading comics since I was a child, when my father got me my first Superman comic. It was something that I could connect with my father about because we didn't have very much else in common. Once he had introduced me to the world of comics, I would ride my bicycle miles down the road to the local store and fully immerse myself in this world. I did fall off the wagon around the time Spider-Man decided to have more clones than adventures, but the superhero movies X-Men and Spider-Man brought me back into the loving embrace of a new comic book. I started the channel Comicstorian in order to share my passion and love for all things comics with likeminded individuals. I never expected to meet and experience even half of what I have, which has led to the creation of this book.

 **JASON**

To say that writing movie reviews about comic book films is my destiny is not something that I would tout as one of my greatest accomplishments but it is certainly very cool. As a child I was always surrounded by great movies. My family is a family of *cinephiles* so I simply played along. As I grew older I learned that it wasn't considered normal to obsess over films, which I thought was odd because people really seem to like movies. All of the pop culture I was exposed to centered on films with branding involving clothes, toys, and video games. Comic book and movie themed birthday parties were common place.

So what's the big deal?

Why is it wrong to discuss ideas about who should be cast as Jean Gray, or who the next Batman villain should be? These are life altering important decisions! In college at Colorado State University I started writing movie reviews on a now defunct website called *The Keen and Hair Reviews* which was my attempt to be the Roger Ebert of the Twenty-First century.

Writing film reviews is unrewarding and serves no real purpose but to be therapeutic. It's also a great way to create rote responses to people who continually ask me my opinions on a new film's. Why are people asking me about my opinion all of the time? It's because I became a full time manager at Grand Slam Sports Cards and Comics in 2008 after my career in teaching social studies was sidelined for numerous reasons. As a person who sits behind the comic counter I immediately become the pop culture expert. In fact it almost becomes my responsibility to see these comic book films first thing when they are released. I would like to say that the majority of the films I've reviewed in this work were at a midnight screening premiere, but I'd be lying.

When Benny the *Comicstorian* walked into my life in early 2014 it was quite interesting. He told me about his YouTubing shenanigans and I was blown away that I met one of these people who claims to make a living off of You-Tube. Shortly after he began to craft his identity of *Comicstorian* and I was asked to come along on the ride.

I created my YouTube identity of Indie-*bookasaurus* and started helping with videos by being in them or even scripting them. I actually have T-Shirts (shameless plug)! During this time I have started a movie review podcast titled *End of the World Movie Reviews* with my friend Andrew Saiger. It is still going and you can check it out if you want the more off color versions of some of these film reviews. All of this somehow leads to me writing movie reviews in this book, which is for a super nerd a great honor.

While I don't hold a degree in being judgmental of cinema I hope you can appreciate the perspective of someone who is a professional at selling comic books and in many ways a professional comic movie reviewer. For some reason my reviews hold weight with some of my customers so I hope they hold some weight with you my dear reader!

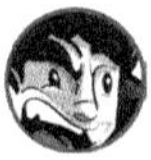

DAN

My name is Dan Rumbles, and I'm the lead editor for the Comicstorian YouTube channel. Sure, I've read a couple of comics here and there throughout the years but it was in

2015, when I became editor for Comicstorian, I really started to read them and gain a lot more appreciation for comics, characters, origins, and more. Some of my favorites include the X-Men, The Guardians of the Galaxy, and The Teen Titans.

The *X-Men* movies were some of my favorite growing up and definitely made me more open to the world of superheroes and comic books. Going back to those *X-Men* movies now, though, I realize how incorrect some of the information was and how some of the movies seemed even better when I didn't know all the details about the mutants.

That being said, many of the movies we've decided to review in this book came out before I became so enveloped in the superhero genre. Because of this, a lot of my movie tastes and opinions have been, maybe understandably, influenced by more recent movies, plots, and special effects, which have evolved drastically over the years. I did my best to watch each movie as though I was watching it around the time it came out and judge its set, action, and special effects accordingly.

While I may be fairly new when it comes to comics and the history of the characters, maybe like some of you, I'd encourage readers to get stuck in, read and watch as much as you can, and you'll soon start learning about what you like.

For this book, I've enjoyed watching the live-action interpretations of comics and worked to deliver some thoughtful opinions on some fantastic superhero franchises that have existed over the years.

 **BENNY**

Before we get started, I want to make it clear that I love some of these movies and hate others. I am very biased when it comes to comic book characters, especially DC. Because of this, I wanted to get the opinions of these two brilliant individuals: regular people like you and me who read a lot of comics and watched a lot of movies. So each section of the book will include our takes on movies that mean so much to us for so many reasons. Some sections will be all three of us weighing in while others might just be one or two voices. The goal is to provide you with enough insight and detail so that you'll enjoy the book and learn something without it feeling too redundant....we hope.

CHAPTER 1:

THE LEGEND OF SUPERMAN

BEHIND THE SCENES: A BIRD, A PLANE, A MAN OF STEEL

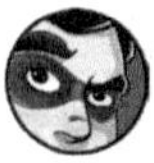

BENNY

To begin, I think having a bit of background about the first movie within the franchise might help us understand the journey the Superman franchise has taken. Here is a collection of the production notes from the first movie in the series.

The first major big-budget superhero feature film, *Superman*, had the challenges of making flying believable, creating special effects without digital animation, and preserving Superman's masculinity while he's wearing tights. But it succeeded, in a big way.

The film rights for *Superman*, based on the DC Comics character introduced in 1938, were bought in 1974 by Pierre Spengler, and Ilya and Alexander Salkind. This team struck a deal with Warner Brothers, originally just for distribution of the film. They decided to film both *Superman* and *Superman II* simultaneously, which proved both exhausting and costly in the long run. Mario Puzo (author of *The Godfather*) wrote both screenplays and delivered them in 1975, but they were considered too long and not a good fit.

Various writing teams were brought in for rewrites until the final version was delivered about a year later. Richard Donner (*The Omen*) became the director. Robert Redford, Burt Reynolds, James Caan, Paul Newman, and several others turned down the Superman role.

After more than 200 auditions, they opted for an unknown actor: Christopher Reeve. Reeve was skinny but determined to build up his body for the part instead of using the muscle suit they designed. David Prowse, who played Darth Vader in the original *Star Wars*, led Reeve's bodybuilding program. Some big name actors were part of the production, including Marlon Brando as Jor-El and Gene Hackman as Lex Luthor. Marlon Brando didn't memorize his movie lines. Instead, he read them off cue cards while filming. In one scene, Brando read from baby Superman's diaper.

Production took 19 months: an estimated year overrun. Superman was filmed at Pinewood Studios and Shepperton Studios in the U.K., plus on-location in Canada, New York, and other U.S. cities. While the film never received an official budget or a timeline, it cost about $55 million to make. The set designs, led by John Barry (known for his production design work on *Star Wars*) and created by over 350 construction workers, were some of the most intricate and expensive of the time. Superman is especially known for its special and visual effects. Completed before the digital age, full-scale models and perfect miniatures were created with elaborate detail.

New filming techniques of the time, like precise and automatic zoom lenses, special camera cranes, and electronic consoles to remotely control filming were used. The opening credits sequence alone cost more than many films at the time.

The biggest challenge was to make the audience believe Superman could fly. No one had flown on screen before without looking silly and obviously fake. Cables and blue and green background screens were used. But it was Christopher Reeve who made it look real. He used his arms in a fluid way and even "banked" around bends during flight. It was a critical part of the story and important for the audience to accept.

The tagline for the movie promotion was simply, "You'll believe a man can fly."

Although production went on (and on), and costs were growing (and growing), Warner Brothers liked what they saw. They added studio money to help fund costs in return for exclusive rights for TV and worldwide distribution. The movie opened during the lucrative Christmas season on December 15, 1978, and went on to gross over $300 million worldwide. The movie was nominated for four Academy Awards, winning for visual effects. *Superman* stayed #1 at the box office for 13 weeks.

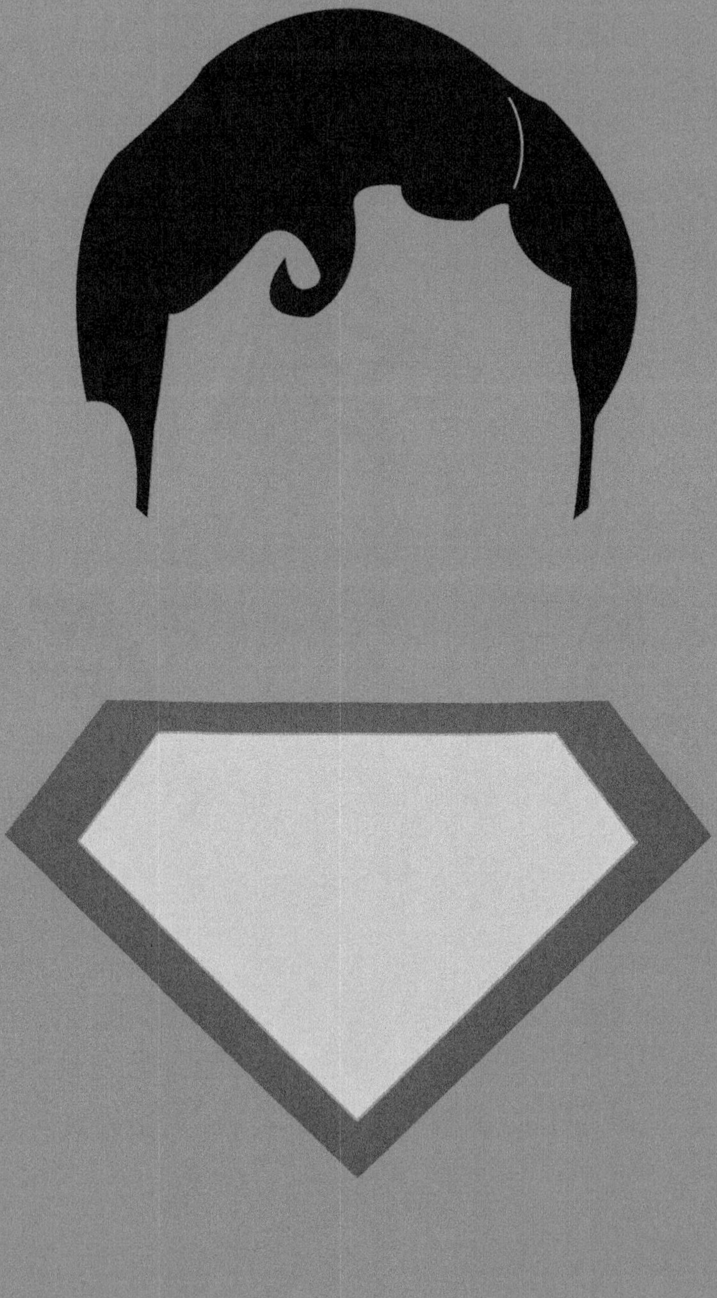

THE FIRST MOVIE

 **BENNY**

Superman as a movie had a lot to live up to as the first big budget superhero film. This being the first Superman film only added to the problems they needed to prepare for. A lot of this was taken into consideration when making the first Superman movie, along with the face that not everyone is fully aware of this character.

The dedication of the intro in the movie to the origin and background story was a huge help in establishing the character of Superman. This was an incredible decision, as it set up the entire franchise with the opening series of events. We knew who Superman was and why he was here. So future movies never needed to touch on these simple facts. We never needed to question things.

This introduction sequence was similar to the Big Bang for the universe. By this I mean, with the explosion of Krypton, big budget superhero movies had begun. No longer were they joke movies, or a movie serial; they were in fact a success.

Looking at the original movie from a more opinion/review standpoint, they had a few challenges in front of them. How do you show destruction on a massive scale and not add a campy look to the film? Their use of miniatures only cemented the destruction of Krypton as a physical tangible explosion.

Too many things are lost to the world of computer animation these days, and seeing the destruction of an entire planet placed on a realistic scale really hammered home its effects after seeing some really good back story which answered some honest to god questions Superman fans have wondered for a while; such as dealing with things such as vanity and pride.

We move to the first appearance of Clark Kent, and Christopher Reeve does an amazing job of separating Clark Kent. He slouches his posture, brings his voice up a few octaves and combs his hair in such a way that the glasses are only the final touch, not the focal point of his transformation.

This is something fans have asked for generations: how does Superman hide himself with glasses? Well it's not just the glasses, it's the whole Clark Kent persona. And as I said, Christopher Reeve shows us that in his portrayal.

Another aspect that is enjoyed by many is Gene Hackmen's portrayal of Lex Luthor. This is a villain that started out as an evil genius out to ruin Superman. But somewhere along the lines he became a villain out to beat up Superman.

This has been shown in his use of power suits, getting powers such as lantern rings, and the use of his own Legion of Doom and Injustice League. But this early portrayal of the villain shows us a version of Lex Luthor that is working towards a real estate scheme. That is literally his plan: buy cheap land and turn it into beach front property so he can be rich. This is classic, cheesy villain 101 and I loved it.

To hammer home the entire experience, Superman does not fight any great super powered bad guys in his battle against Luthor Real Estate. Instead, he has to fight against the disasters Luthor's missiles are causing. Dams exploding, cars piling up, and bridges crumbling are all the kind of things people forgot Superman stops. They always expect Doomsday or Brainiac, but Superman's goal is to promote truth, liberty and the American way. Fun fact: "The American Way," was in his slogan in this day and age.

During this time, Superman was being established as doing more than punching things. He was growing to represent more: to be a thinker with power.

What I'm getting at is that this is one of if not the best Superman movie in the entire collection of Superman movies. It does the best job of portraying Superman without bogging everything down.

All of my favorite moments and comic portrayals aside, the movie boasted an impressive screenplay that was smart while maintaining the humor. The music was also to none with the Superman theme becoming famous and instantly recognizable the world over.

As you can see by looking anywhere on the internet, many fans enjoy this original *Superman* movie. While you can see its age poking through, it does stand the test of time. So with such a promising start, how did the franchise begin to falter? At what point did a Superman movie become something to skip and watch on television?

When did a movie titled *Man of Steel* bring back the franchise and gross around six hundred and sixty-eight million dollars in the box office? Well the road from a three hundred-million-dollar box office to sixty- eight million dollars is a long one that we'll dive into.

 **JASON**

The Superman film franchise is important to recognize because it was the first time when film techniques established by *2001: A Space Odyssey* and *Star Wars: A New Hope* were used in mainstream movies to propel images from comic books to the silver screen. This franchise had staggering success followed by a slow and steady decline over the course of a decade.

What cannot be denied is the influence this franchise has on all other comic book franchises; its lessons of what to do and what not to do. As a child of the 1980s I grew up on the Americana of the first three Superman films and was profoundly influenced by their achievements and shortcomings. What follows are my thoughts on these films in individual reviews.

The film that started off the modern superhero genre, *Superman*, lives up to all of the hype, using elements of great filmmaking from the 1970s. This is one of my favorite films because it incorporates great elements of film and lives up to the promise of what a movie can be.

The script by Mario Puzo established the key elements that are needed in an origin film and gave Superman the air of an American myth from the get-go. Everything taking place on the last days of Krypton embodies an intense amount of imagination, establishing villains for future. Jor-El is played masterfully by the greatest actor of the 20th Century, Marlon Brando.

The film is slow paced following the destruction of Krypton. Experiencing the childhood of Clark Kent on screen shows the distinct juxtaposition of the alien world of Krypton and the

Americana of Smallville. It's important that this film shows Clark Kent as an alien becoming an American—a key character element of Superman throughout the franchise.

Christopher Reeve, Margot Kidder, and Gene Hackman are the gold standard that will always stand the test of time in the comic book genre. John Williams' score married with Richard Donner's photography, which creates emotional and rousing scenes that showed the beauty of stories based on comic books, are some of the best elements of the film.

This is a film that is only diminished by the time it was filmed in, when action sequences were much more difficult to orchestrate. The Richard Donner director's cut is worth the viewing, as you will believe in Superman by the end of the film.

The Superman movies had quite the roller coaster in the success department. They started out high, went low, and then ended up back on top.

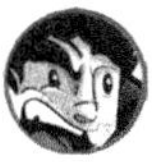

DAN

Superman kicked the franchise off strong. Beginning the film with the origin of Krypton and Kal-El was perfect. It set up *Superman* and *Superman II* in a short, concise manner. Christopher Reeve proved to be a perfect Superman, portraying both the roles of Clark Kent and Superman in a dynamic way that showed the differences in the two characters was more than just glasses and a suit.

Reeve's managed to show these characters did have different personalities and demeanors, giving the audience reason to believe the two weren't one in the same. Reeve also did a great job at making the flying somewhat believable. Sure, it was obviously fake, but the way he moved around in the sky made you really think that he was flying and not just floating around on wires.

Gene Hackman was a good Lex Luthor, portraying him as an evil genius, who had plans to make himself rich, even if it meant the death of others. The character was at least somewhat realistic because he didn't use crazy machines to complete his plot.

My biggest problem with the original Superman was that it ended in a way that just didn't feel like a resolution. It was almost as if they decided to use a shortcut to get the ending. It was good, but it could've been better. Overall, this was definitely the best Superman movie from the first four in the franchise. *Superman* set the bar high, giving *Superman II* some big spandex to fill.

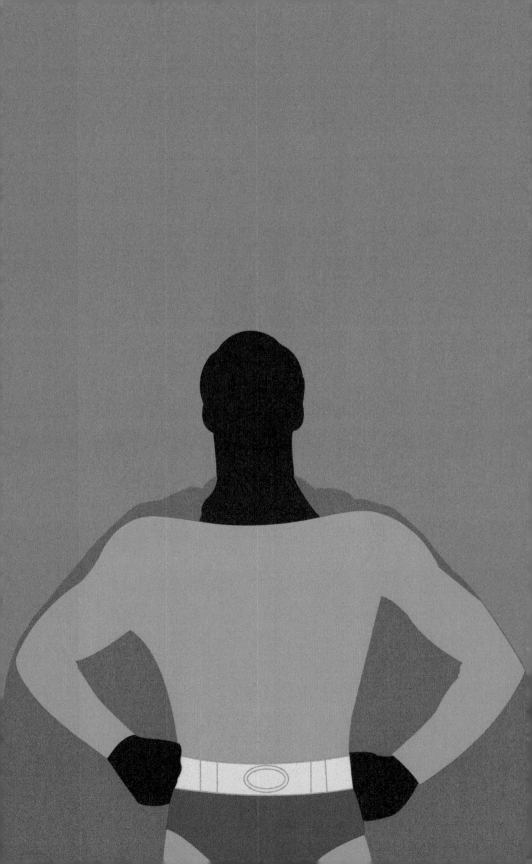

SUPERMAN 2

 **BENNY**

This brings us to the next movie, *Superman II*. Now it's odd that originally these were both intended to be filmed at the same time. Because with the shift in director, and a few cast change ups like Marlon Brando leaving his role of Jor-El, we are left with a different type of Superman film.

This isn't the beginning of the end, but it's a sign of things to come. The pacing holds with the beautiful dialogue and new director Richard Lester's unique brand of humor brought a new element to the story. It's not like the original Superman. Its tone is more light hearted to match his style of romantic comedies, but that's what makes it great. You don't just feel like you are watching the same Superman movie. You walk out of *Superman II* feeling like you learned a little more about the character: a new side and a twist that you weren't expecting.

To top it off, the increased budget is immediately noticeable with the larger stunts and the villains actually having Super powers as well. Since the first movie didn't have any superhero fighting, you could have easily made this movie with nothing more than punching, wires and green screen and no one would have questioned you. But Richard Lester went for a full-out fight in the middle of Metropolis. It's not quite on the level of destruction in *Man of Steel*, but it does give you a good feeling of Superpowers.

Regardless of how Richard Lester did with the movie, the production as rife with controversies that to this day are still debated. Richard Donner, the original director, was pulled off of the project for unknown reasons (each side telling their own version of the story). While this doesn't sound like a big deal at first, Richard Donner had completed 75% of the movie before leaving its production.

The new director, which was Richard Lester, needed to film 51% of the movie to actually get the directors credit. So he reshot many of the original scenes Richard Donner already shot. In the end, the movie wasn't along the original idea that Richard Donner had. For years fans clamored for the original again. It wasn't until 2006 that we would get a recut version of the film restoring many of Richard Donners original scenes. But the controversy was still there, and it was a sign of problems to come.

 **JASON**

The first sequel of *Superman*, *Superman II*, was carefully assembled, showing how to continue an origin story with thoughtful character development. Richard Donner was originally set to direct both *Superman* & *Superman II* together. However, in the middle of production Donner was replaced with Richard Lester, whose comedic background changed the tone of the film from its previous film.

Even with that mostly disastrous change this is a superb sequel that shows Kal-El struggling to reconcile his personal life with his role as the sole hero of planet Earth.

The story of Superman sacrificing his powers for the woman he loves (Lois Lane) will be used in many superhero stories to come. It has rightfully earned its place in film history. The superhero battle of General Zod and his lieutenants verses Superman is bar none one of the best super fights, even though it is not as fast paced as the action sequences that we see in film today.

While the end of the story has some bizarre displays of powers, Superman using his chest emblem to incapacitate an opponent and erasing Lois Lane's knowledge of Superman's identity with a "super kiss," there are many parts of this film that have been used in superhero sequels even today. I always enjoy the scene in the diner where Clark Kent actually takes vengeance on the bully. The comedic beat that follows is priceless.

Christopher Reeve plays the dual identities of Kal-El so well that it has not been matched in any of the other movies of this storied franchise.

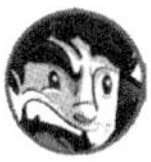

DAN

Superman II seemed to have two main plots: General Zod and his goal to rule all and the relationship between Clark and Lois. This film had a lighter tone to it than its predecessor, especially in the scenes between Lois and Clark. It was clear that *Superman II* was its own movie and not a reskinned *Superman*, and I like that. However, there were many odd components to this sequel that raised questions that were never answered.

New abilities and powers were added to the story. Some were kind of cool, but it was never revealed how and why these existed. For example, the plastic "S" that Superman pulled off his chest and hurled made no sense and seemed out of place. I will say that, for its time when superhero films were new, *Superman II* is a pretty good film and worth watching. I'd recommend you stop there and not continue watching the remaining films in this part of the franchise.

THE MAKING OF A TRILOGY

 BENNY

Next on the list is *Superman III,* and this is where things became a problem. It's a story of Superman versus Brainiac and Mr. Mxyzptlk. It also has an under lying plot with Supergirl arriving and becoming a love interest for Superman! Well, it was supposed to: that was the original script submitted to Warner Bros. before they rejected it and had their own disaster created.

Superman III came out in 1983 right when the world was dealing with the technology boom. Things like *Tron* had come out to critical acclaim and in response Warn Bros. wanted a technology heavy Superman story. So we followed Richard Pryor as computer genius Gus Gorman and his creation of a synthetic kryptonite. The kryptonite didn't weaken Superman as expected. Instead, it created an evil Superman. This Superman wasn't even truly evil. He was just plain mean.

The movie is known for its poor humor and campy nature, which was achieved by bringing in Richard Pryor. He was a well-known comedian at the time which led a lot of people to wonder why they bring him in. There was a growing fear the next Superman movie was fall into a pit of camp and feel like the 1966 Batman movie based on the television show.

Another well-known issue is the attempt to replace Lex Luthor with Ross Webster. Word spread like wildfire, and we were stuck with a mess of a Superman movie that barely grossed eighty million: only double its budget. Warner Bros. wasn't too happy about this.

A few things happened before we got to the fourth film. Since the movie did so poorly, the producers at the time —Alexander and Ilya Salkind— decided that the Superman movie franchise had run its course. This was confirmed by the failure of the *Supergirl* movie. The movie was supposed to freshen up the Superman franchise with a fresh female lead. Instead, it grossed only half of its budget and was a complete failure. Because of this, they sold the rights to Superman movies to Menahem Golan and Yoram Globus, who were all set to get Superman back on track.

The public voted with their wallets. When the fourth film in the franchise came out, it was directly affected by the poor response that *Superman III* got. The movie didn't even cross forty million dollars. Jon Cryer, who played the role of Lennie Luthor, explained some of what happened years later in a career retrospective. He explained that they had no money to make the movie. The funds kept getting moved around until they couldn't even afford the craft table. Before the movie came out, he met with Christopher Reeve and warned him that the movie was going to be bad. He wanted the movie to do well so that it could be a revival of Superman,v but it wasn't going to be.

 **JASON**

Superman III is basically Superman vs. Computers! It's funny to revisit this movie that I adored as a child. It's crazy to see how much it would drive me up a wall if it were released today. Christopher Reeve reprised his role, carrying the franchise, which struggled without the guidance of the masterful storytelling of Mario Puzo. Instead we see Superman for what the public believed the comic books to be, a "funny book."

Richard Lester took full control of the helm incorporating so many comedic moments; it's very sad to see how far this franchise fell from its glorious beginnings. How could it not be comedic? Richard Pryor's Gus Gormon character takes center stage as the accidental villain, becoming used by a stooge-like trio of villains. While the comedy beats had worked in the previous films they could not balance the serious scope of a Superman tale with the goofy and laughable evil plot of controlling the world with confounded evil computers! This is worth the watch just to see what Hollywood writers thought could be done with computers in the dawn of the Information Age.

Not everything in this movie is awful however. Superman freezes a lake and drops it on a burning nuclear facility, which while cheesy, is still totally awesome! Annette O'Toole plays Lana Lang, Clark Kent's old flame from high school, and making us see Superman's humanity as he cannot help but fall in love with her.

My favorite scene, though it makes little sense, is when Superman has a contest of wills against himself after being "poisoned" by synthesized Kryptonite. This scene is often quoted and fondly remembered as it shows the range of Christopher Reeve. In the end, the film cannot be salvaged.

The awful final climactic battle against the "super computer" is unforgivable even for its day.

In many ways this was the death knell for the Superman film franchise; we just wouldn't know it until the next movie.

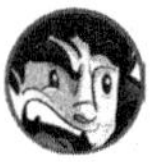

DAN

Superman III was when things started to get bad, and I mean real bad. The movie starts off rather slow, with no clear plot. Computer Genius Gus gets blackmailed by the bad guys to create a synthetic Kryptonite to be used to get Superman out of the picture. The synthetic Kryptonite doesn't work like the real stuff; instead of weakening Superman, it just made him evil. Huh? But the weird part was that Superman wasn't really evil, but more of a huge jerk to everyone. It was also resolved in a manner that, once again, rose questions that were not adequately answered. The studio should've ended the movie series here since they apparently didn't know what they were doing anymore. But no, they didn't stop. They went on to make *Superman IV*.

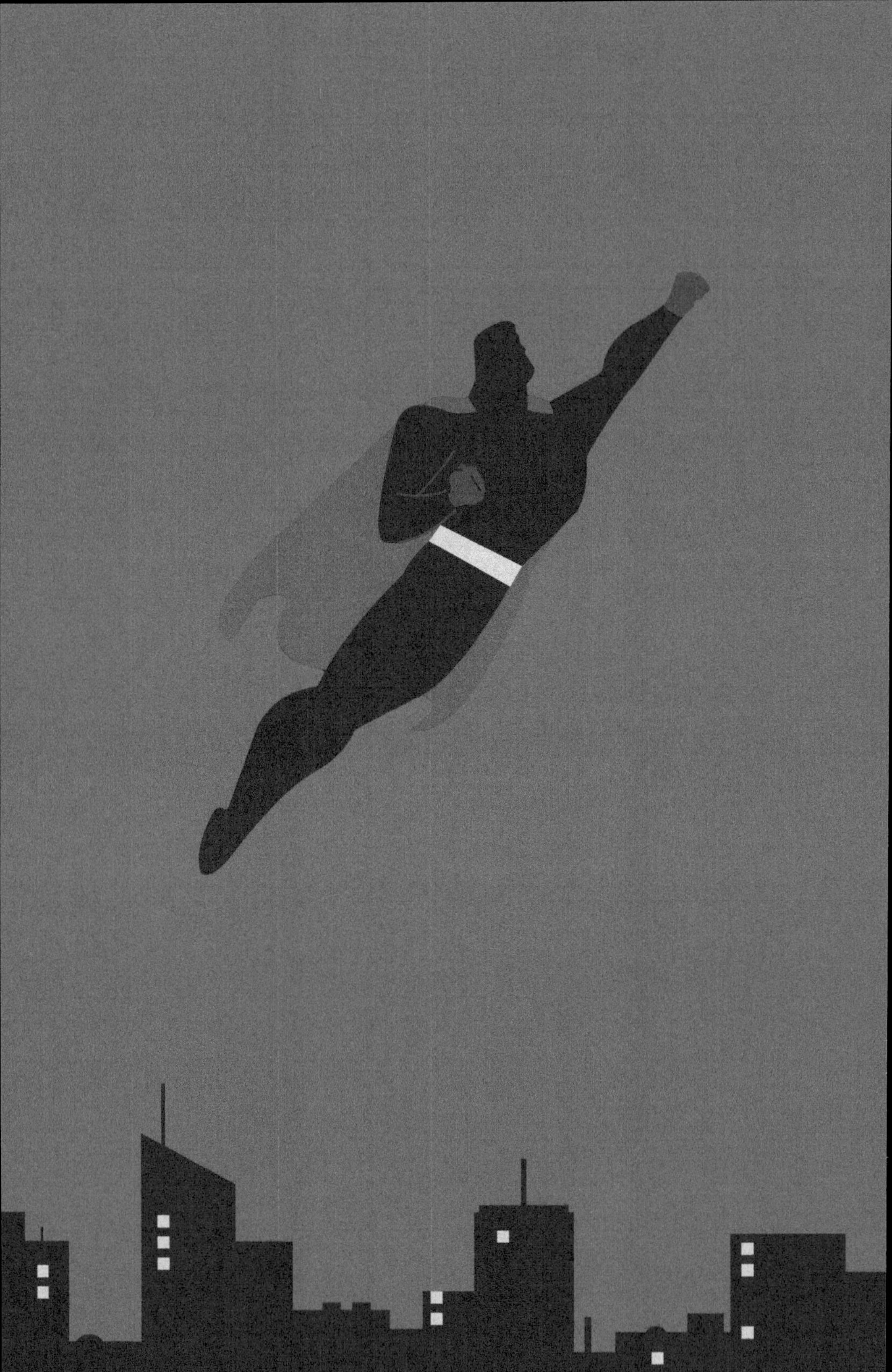

THE QUEST FOR PEACE

 **BENNY**

Superman IV tries a sort of reboot in a day when they didn't happen. It killed off Superman's parents, introduced his Kryptonian mother, changed the owner of the *Daily Planet* and even broke Lex Luthor out of jail using his nephew Lenny Luthor. It tried to get across the message that Nuclear Power was bad by pitting Superman against a new villain: Nuclear Man. The whole thing did a very good job of sealing the fate of franchise.

There were many talks about a *Superman V* to revive the series. It also carried the name *Superman: The New Movie.* It was going to tell the story of Superman's death and revival in the bottled city of Kandor. But after the poor response to *Superman III* and the commercial failure of *Superman IV*, they canceled the movie.

It was after the success of the comic series *The Death Of Superman* that things looked hopeful again. In 1993, Warner Bros. purchased the film rights to Superman and handed the project to producer Jon Peters. They had no interest in using anything from the previous Superman regime. They had an entire new script written to get away from *Superman: The New Movie.*

 **JASON**

I can sum up my opinions on *Superman IV* in two simple words, "Oh No!" The film starts with the noblest of goals and turns into a disaster. It's a bona fide classic, bad comic book movie. The first act of the film revisits what was popular from the first two films and missing from *Superman III*. Right away, there is a return of favorite characters and the musical theme of John Williams. It's still a treat to see Christopher Reeve reprising his role as Superman and Clark Kent. All of this nostalgia takes a nosedive when poor special effects and an awful storyline take over.

While the plot of the film plays like the first two with Lex Luthor wanting to kill Superman and get rich while doing it, we are subjected to John Cryer's Lenny who is one of the worst screen lackey's to date—I still avoid *Two and a Half Men* because of it. The final act of the movie is so rushed together and badly edited that it's worth watching for how comically bad it is.

In a span of twenty minutes Superman is mortally wounded by Nuclear Man, becomes sick, and loses his gray hair. He's dying for reasons unknown (no kryptonite was harmed in the making of this film). Suddenly, with an energy source from the beginning of the film Superman is back and ready to defend Lacy Warfield, the girl whose picture he saw in the newspaper, from Nuclear Man. What follows is the most awful superhero fight scene portrayed on the silver screen I have seen in a long time.

The effects were bad back in 1987, and look even worse on Blu-ray. Nuclear Man, who has "nuclear hot" skin, picks Lacy up and flies her through the atmosphere into outer space.

You'll be asking yourself, "What were these guys thinking while they were filming this?" In the end, Superman triumphs but it leaves the viewer saying "oh no," just like John Cryer does several times. Watch this at your own peril.

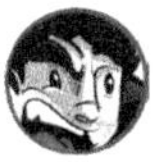

DAN

Superman IV: The Quest for Peace was made during the height of the nuclear scares, very evident in the plot's focus to remove nuclear threats from the world. Of course, Lex Luthor used this for his own gain and brought on the first engineered, super-powered human. This film, however, had much of the plot focused on the Daily Planet's change in ownership. While this concept was a good idea, it was poorly executed. They went overboard with Superman's powers, implying that there was simply nothing he couldn't do. I mean, he had wall-rebuilding eye beams for goodness sake! While *Superman IV* was better than its predecessor, unfortunately, it wasn't by much.

NICOLAS CAGE'S SUPERMAN REBORN

 **BENNY**

The first attempt to revive the franchise was *Superman Reborn*. Supposedly it was going to aim at being family friendly in the same vein as *Batman Forever* with toy companies getting on board as early as the screenplay. The story would feature Superman professing his love to Lois Lane before dying at the hands of Doomsday. Then, his life force would be reborn in Lois as a virgin birth and become 21 in 3 weeks, allowing him to save the world.

It was rejected for sharing similar ideas to Batman's underlying themes of heroism in "Batman Forever" (because that was the only problem with the idea of a reborn Superman). The rewrite for *Superman Reborn* involved Doomsday infused with Kryptonian blood, Superman having romance problems, and Brainiac stealing Superman's corpse. Superman would eventually revive and use a robot suit to mimic his powers before learning a system similar to the Force to relearn his powers. Suffice to say, it get greenlit.

After both of these were rejected, another attempt was made with the *Superman Lives* movie, a film that Kevin Smith was brought on to help. He has an entire video explaining the story behind it, but suffice to say it contained robotic spiders, Brainiac with polar bears, and Nicolas Cage was tied-in as Clark.

It was becoming evident that Warner Bros really didn't know what to do with their big-name characters Batman and Superman at this point. You can see this in their script attempts that completely rewrite characters, concepts and themes of the heroes they are focused on.

I personally feel this is a mentality started from the original *Batman* movie, and I explain that further in our Batman chapter. But the short version is: *Batman* became popular regardless of whether or not it matched the comic book lore established over decades. Ever since then, movie studios seemed to be more concerned with telling their own stories and not the ones that comic fans wanted.

SUPERMAN RETURNS

 *JASON*

After a very long time, we had the fifth film in the franchise, *Superman Returns*. There was a mighty struggle to get the fifth film in the Superman franchise produced. There have been great stories about the painful process. At the end of the day, was this film worth the wait?

While the production value was great at the time *Superman Returns*, brought to us by Bryan Singer, it failed to live up to the franchise of the past. The film tried to capture the nostalgia of the old films, but it was truly a pale comparison to the epic films created by Mario Puzo's scripts. Instead it felt derivative of the previous films, lacking the inspiration Superman should instill in viewers.

Central to my dislike of this film is Brandon Routh's portrayal of the Man of Steel. While he played a heroic Superman he failed at showing the dual identity of Kal-El that Christopher Reeve masterfully portrayed even in the franchise's darkest moments. The film did touch upon the idea of Superman having a son, something never fully explored in the comics— nor in the film. It was hinted that this would be revisited in future films but clearly they went in a different direction

We're not sure where this movie fits into the overall franchise. It is implied that this took place directly after *Superman II*, which ignores the other films. Explicitly not explaining where this film takes place in the storyline confuses the audience.

This could have been explained easily in the beginning by mentioning that he left Earth after his battle with General Zod. This film is a true disappointment given the importance of Superman to our popular culture.

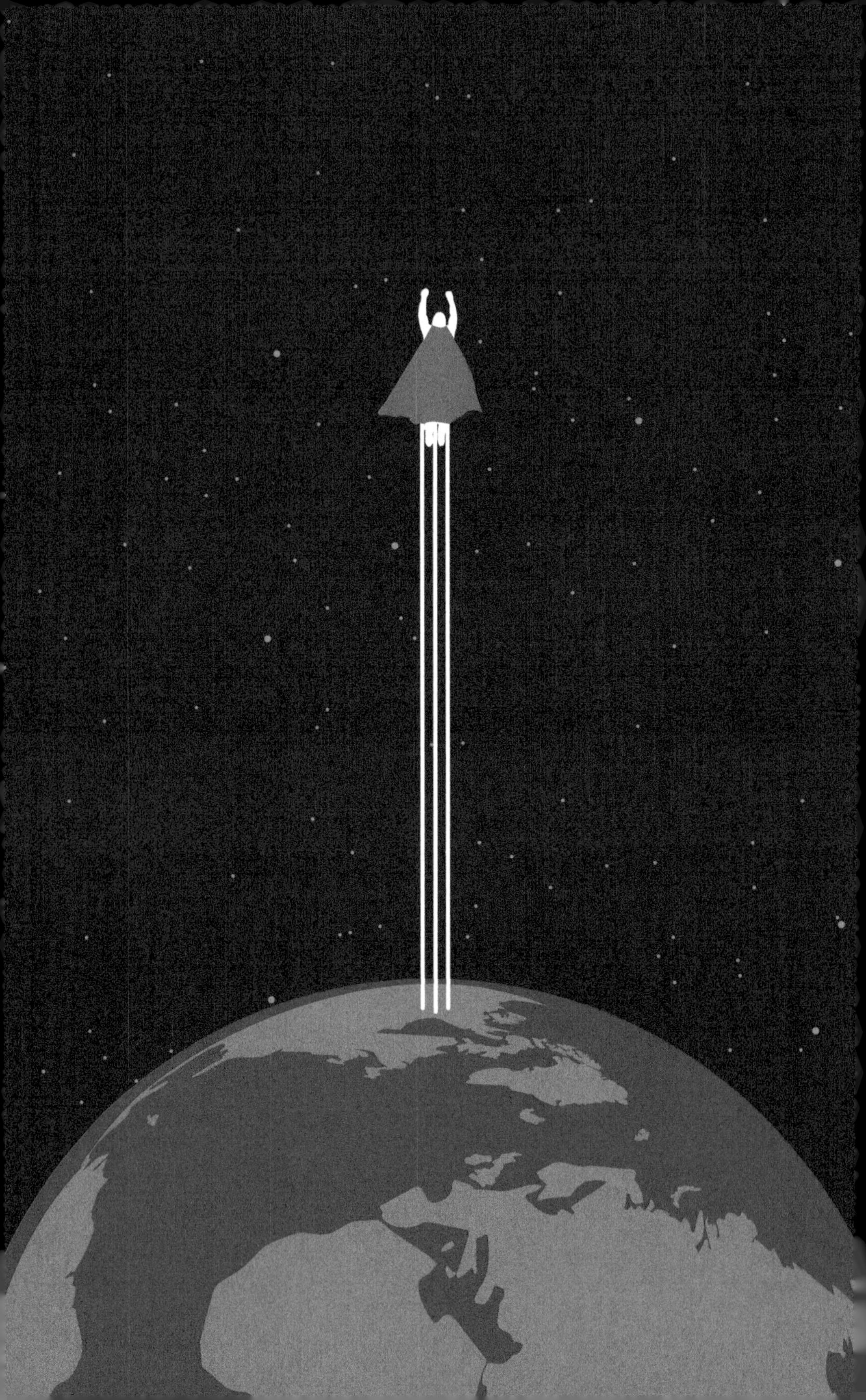

MAN OF STEEL

 BENNY

It was in 2008 that Warner Bros. decided they should reboot the character of Superman. As successful as *Superman Returns* was, it was trying to rebuild a franchise that was long dead. With a reboot, they could bring a grittier, edgier Superman (one that would match up with the ideas of the Marvel Cinematic Universe). But there was a little more going on behind the scenes. Warner Bros was in constant legal battles with Jerry Siegel's family over their attempts at recapturing the rights to Superman.

The courts ruled that Warner Bros. didn't owe any back royalties for the previous movies. It was decided that they needed to start a new movie before 2011 or they would be liable to be sued again by the family for lost revenue.

Regardless of why they pushed forward with it, things were finally in motion for a DC extended universe. The public was tired of single movies showing the adventures of self-contained Superhero worlds. Opening up these movies to a larger, more extended universe allowed for possibilities, story devices and lore beyond "Superman saved the day!" It also allowed the director to put in countless easter eggs to start the DC Extended Universe.

The film came out hot on the tail of the Marvel Cinematic Universe being in full swing, and it benefited greatly. The movie-going public was ready for a modern day Superman.

A gritty one, a little more realistic and, controversially, one that would kill people. It wasn't one hundred percent accepted across the board. Fans of the classic Superman loved to argue that Superman wouldn't kill (even if it was General Zod). Regardless, it was a commercial and financial success. Bringing in over six hundred and sixty-eight million MADE it the most successful Superman in the franchise's history.

While this is far from the billion-dollar success of the *Avengers*, it's a very good start when you place it into context. The first film in the Marvel Cinematic Universe was *Iron Man*, and it grossed five hundred and eighty-five dollars. While *Man of Steel* was riding the success of the currently successful Avengers franchise, it was what DC fans had wanted for a long time. A Superman version of the recent *Dark Knight Trilogy*, though a tad less human.

As for my persona opinions on the movie: I love it. To counter the argument of individuals being unhappy with Superman's behavior or his willingness to kill, I tell them read more than the classic Superman. There are multiple versions of the hero, some of which willingly kill and some that are a lot darker and broodier.

The film managed to humanize a godlike character, but not in the way that states: "oh, Superman is just like us." Rather, in a manner in which we would actually act if an alien godlike being appeared before us. Is he here for good or evil? It does an amazing job of making it feel like it could happen next you, but keeping an air of space combat and travel. The idea that Clark deals with the dual ideals of his parents is one of the elements I truly enjoyed in this movie.

The idea IS that Jor-El didn't just send him here because it was convenient, but with a purpose. That purpose, of course, is completely against what Jonathan Kent wants his son to do, which is stay safe and hidden.

 **JASON**

The comic book film genre received a shot in the arm from 2008's *Iron Man* and *The Dark Knight*. Now it was time to revisit Superman with *Man of Steel*. Superman, once the pinnacle of superheroes, had seen reduced sales in the comic book industry. Writers constantly grappled with the difficulties of writing a story about a character that is nearly unbeatable. Visionary director Zack Snyder fought to honor the images from comics and bring them to a wider audience.

His success with *300* and *Watchmen* showed that he knew how to bring superheroes to life so it was with great anticipation that I went into this film. It is a shame that I found this film to be endlessly disappointing. So what is wrong with this film? The opening scenes on Krypton were imaginative and mind blowing. Krypton was a more fascinating alien world; it was something out of a Star Wars movie!

After a very exciting opening—an homage to Mario Puzo's opening of *Superman: The Movie*—it loses a lot of momentum.

The script begins to see-saw back and forth, juxtaposing the current life of Kal-El with his upbringing. This non-linear storytelling is a clear departure from traditional comic book origins and attempts to deliver powerful scenes without any real through line. However, the theme of his upbringing on

Earth is actually a world of mistrust and danger. His parents are scared of what "they" might do to Clark if "they" ever found out. I found this fear to be unfounded because that is not the world that I'm familiar with, having grown up in in the Midwestern United States—presumably the area where Clark grew up in Smallville—myself.

In fact, Jonathan Kent dies in a tornado just to keep Clark's secret. This is a clear departure from the Puzo script where Clark realizes he is powerless to do anything about his father's death. He could obviously save his father in *Man of Steel* but why didn't he? Out of fear?

It seems like a selfish reason for a man who is supposed to represent selflessness. But this is a very different Superman from the Shuster and Siegel comics as we see throughout the rest of the film. This point of contention is in the very character of Superman, who used to be representative of "truth, justice, and the American way." It makes the rest of the film highly unwatchable despite the stunning visuals and eye candy. I did not believe in this Superman, but perhaps he is a Superman for a different generation and I am just nostalgic for the Superman of the Twentieth Century.

I recognize and celebrate the original films of Superman as being the "gold standard" of the superhero film genre. While there was a steep decline in later films, it never ruined the original experience. However, as more films are released it seems as though Hollywood does not understand what made Superman work.

In many ways it was Christopher Reeve and his total understanding of the dual identity that makes those original Superman films so important to me as a viewer. It is the feeling of optimism that permeates throughout those original films that makes Superman so highly re-watchable. Until modern day filmmakers can depart from the dark reality that they want to embrace in their films, I'm afraid that Superman will not be the comic book icon that he once was.

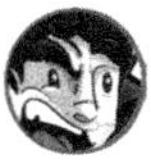

DAN

Man of Steel came and stole my heart for best Superman film. It used a lot of flashbacks to give an idea of what it's like to grow up as Superman: adjusting to powers and knowing if and when to use them. The origin story told in *Man of Steel* was incredibly in-depth and made you understand the character.

The film showed what things were like on the planet of Krypton, explained the family shields that would later become the iconic Superman "S," and displayed the complex relationship between Zod and Jor-El and how alike they actually were in some aspects. Yes, there were parts of the origin story that were obscure and different from what I know, but it was done well.

I think what makes *Man of Steel* my favorite of the Superman films was that it seemed more realistic, especially from how it showed the superhero grow up. Many times with Clark, the focus is on being a child in Smallville to Superman in Metropolis, rarely touching on the in between. *Man of Steel* really touched on the in between, showing how his powers developed and how Superman helped people while avoiding revealing his identity. It was a cool side to the character that you rarely get to see.

As the movie went on though, some things did start to get a little too different, which had me concerned. But, in the end, they were done well and worked with the story. This fifth film in the series actually changed how I look at Superman. Out of the entire franchise, *Man of Steel* is the one I'd recommend most, followed by the original 1978 Superman—a great film to start the franchise.

While the quality of the Superman movie franchise went on quite the rollercoaster, at the end of it all, it ended up back on top.

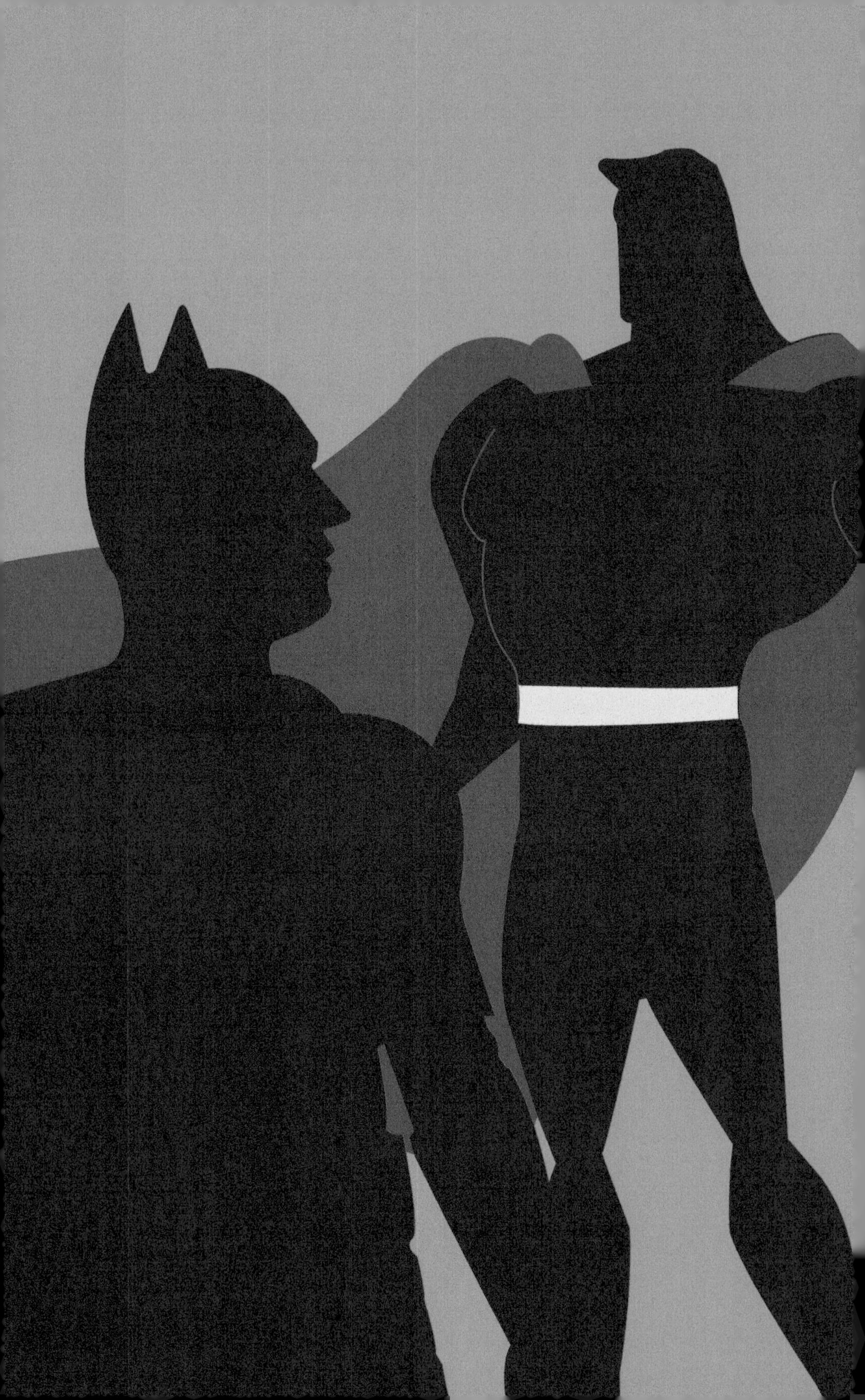

BATMAN v SUPERMAN

 **BENNY**

This brings us to the final movie within the franchis: *Batman v Superman*: *Dawn of Justice.* This one was released just before we wrapped up this chapter, and everyone on the writing team for this book felt it was something we needed to include. Originally, *Batman v Superman* was supposed to be a *Man of Steel* sequel. But it didn't stay that way for very long.

The first announcements claimed the director and screen writer would return for the sequel, and it would come out around 2015. A month later, Zack Snyder announced at Comic-Con that this would feature the first meeting of Batman and Superman in cinematic format. In my opinion, this is what started *Batman v Superman* on the path it took: one of mashed together movies and a severe flow problem.

But we will have to discuss what happened next in Warner Bros.' race to get an *Avengers*-style movie out in the Batman segment of this book.

A FINAL LOOK BEHIND THE CAPE

 **BENNY**

As you can see from both the opinions of a newer comic book reader (Dan) and an old nostalgia viewer (Jason), there are vastly differing opinions on Superman. While they agree on a few elements, *Man of Steel* completely divided the fan base by what each really wanted. Did they want the classic Superman of 1978, or the Superman that wasn't really wanted by the world he protected? Maybe they wanted the comical Superman of *Superman III*— though I doubt anyone really did. We'll have to wait and see how Superman continues to evolve in the upcoming Justice League films. But for now, all that's left IS to sit back, plug in the VCR, and binge the old animated series.

CHAPTER 2:

Enter the Dark Knight

 **BENNY**

In a world of superhero comics, *Batman* is unique. Without being a mutant and with no superhuman powers, Batman is a brilliant detective, self-appointed crime fighter, and a superb athlete. He's also a millionaire with a dark past.

The Batman character was introduced in May 1939 in Detective Comics issue #27 as Bat-Man. An Illustrator and cartoon artist, Bob Kane, was commissioned by DC Comics to invent a superhero. Kane, along with writer Bill Finger, created the Batman character, his backstory, disguise, Gotham City, the villains, and more.

In 1979, Michael Uslan and Benjamin Melniker purchased the film rights for Batman from DC Comics. The goal was to create the definitive, dark version of Batman (the way the character was originally intended). Columbia Pictures and United Artists were turned down as studios to make the film because they wanted a campy movie styled on the 1960s TV show.

It was announced that the movie had a $15 million budget at the 1980 Comic Art Convention in New York, even though no studio had committed. Soon after, Warner Bros. Studio was accepted to make the film. The original screenplay, developed by Sam Hamm, was changed many times. Anton Furst was hired as production designer to create the all-important Batman environment, and Danny Elfman wrote the film's musical score.

After the success of *Beetlejuice*, Tim Burton was brought on to direct *Batman*. Mel Gibson was the original choice for the lead role, but he was committed to filming *Lethal Weapon 2*. Pierce Brosnan, Tom Selleck, and others were considered. In the end, Michael Keaton was hired to star as Batman. Comic books fans sent an estimated 50,000 letters to Warner Bros. protesting the choice to have a comedic actor play the part of Batman. Bob Kane was hired as a creative consultant to try and combat the perception that this movie would be silly or light in any way.

Willem Dafoe, David Bowie, James Woods, and Robin Williams were considered for the role of the Joker. Robin Williams even accepted the role, but he was released when Jack Nicholson finally agreed to play the part. Jack Nicholson negotiated a stake of the profits and merchandising from *Batman*, earning him about $60 million – still the highest amount paid for an actor in a movie. Other actors included: Kim Basinger as Gotham Globe photographer Vicki Vale, Jack Palance as crime boss Carl Grissom, Pat Hingle as Commissioner Gordon, and Lee Wallace as Gotham City's Mayor Borg.

Critical to achieving the vision for *Batman* was the creation of a dark and ominous environment for the story. Filming was highly secretive and all on-location in England. The nightmarish New York set was built using most of the 18 soundstages at Pinewood Studios. The Wayne Manor exterior was filmed at Knebworth House north of London, and the interior of the Manor was filmed at Hatfield House (also the mansion in *Lara Croft: Tomb Raider*).

The Batmobile was 20 feet long with an 8 foot wheelbase, weighed a ton and a half, and was built on the frame of a Chevy Impala. The film's cathedral scene was a model built 38-feet tall that cost $100,000. Batman's Batsuit was sculpted from all-black latex, and it cost $250,000 to create a range of different capes and heads to be used.

Given that the goal was to intimidate, tights, spandex, and underpants were ruled out. Special effects didn't play a large role in the film, but Anton Furst's elaborate sets, sleek Batmobile, and transformed Batman logo—along with Danny Elfman's film score—helped create the film's menacing environment.

Batman isn't entirely accurate when compared to the comic books. Fans were outraged when Vickie Vale, a blonde in the movie but a redhead in the comic due to a coloring error in printing, was escorted by Bruce Wayne's butler, Alfred, into the Batcave. In addition, a few characters were left out (or added) and other anomalies. There was also anger at changing the murderer of Bruce Wayne's parents from Joe Chill to the Joker. Because of these fundamental deviations, director Tim Burton received a lifelong ban from any and all Comic-Con events.

The marketing and promotion of *Batman* followed the template set by *Star Wars* for the modern-day blockbuster. Promotional and cross-marketing via toys, T-shirts, fast food promotions, and countless merchandising added to the build-up of the movie's release.

Batman grossed $411 million worldwide, taking in $43 million in the first three days alone in the U.S., and broke single-day records every day of its opening weekend. The original budget was $35 million rising to an estimated $48 million in total. The top grossing movie in 1989, the promotional tagline was

"Only one will claim the night." *Batman* won an Academy Award for Best Art Direction.

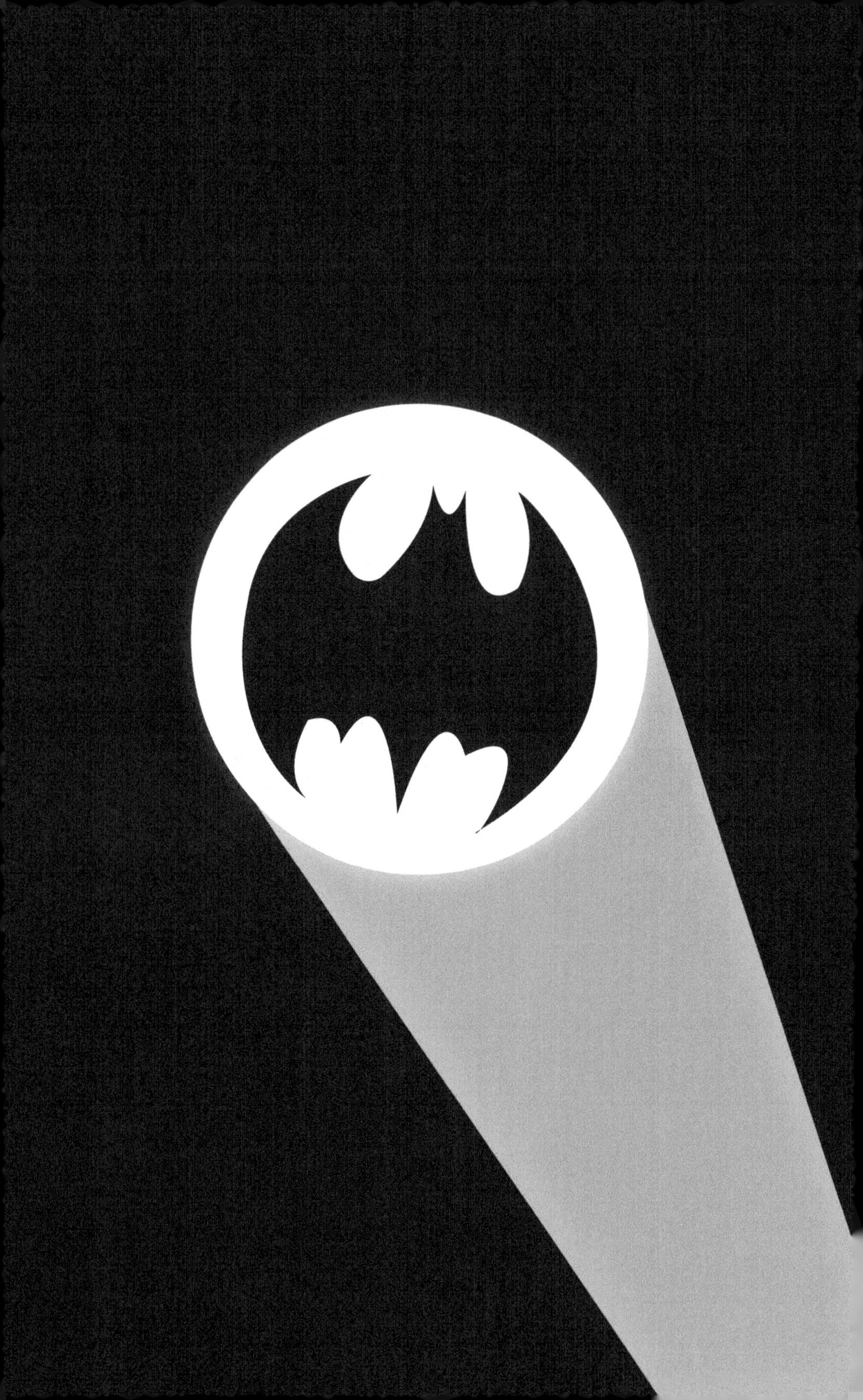

A City That Needed Batman

 **BENNY**

By bringing in Tim Burton, they ensured that they were going to get a dark and moody Batman movie. Comic books were already taking this shift by allowing individuals such as Frank Miller to reinvent the character for their own stories. This feeling of a dark and gloomy Batman was carried over into the film's environments, bringing us a dark and gloomy Gotham. One ripped straight from the pages it was born in, a city seemingly void of good hard working people. One that is overrun by the crime lord Carl Grissom, with a police force owned by the gangs instead of fighting for the people of Gotham.

This was a city that needed Batman instead of the city for Batman to joke in. This movie was dark and moody, but also funny and smart. The wit given off by the characters kept you feeling like this was a comic book movie. The portrayal of the Joker by Jack Nicholas was phenomenal, and I think what started the trend of Batman movies being about the villains and not Batman.

But as much as I love this Batman—and I tell everyone that they need to watch it—I feel as though it started out decline in superhero movies. As we stated in our production notes, some fundamental things in the Batman lore were changed to make a better story for Tim Burton to tell, which in turn made a successful movie. That none of these changes were needed and is the core of the issues many fans have with the movie. But while Superman stayed very true to the proper Superman mythos with his first movie, *Batman* proved that not every superhero film needed to do that.

It proved that changing a few things was potentially a good move, because why would people want a true to comic movie? This is something that would stick with comic book movies for almost two decades, but most notably with the Batman franchise itself.

 **JASON**

Although watching Batman on syndicated television growing up in the 1980s was a joy, it was different from what was going on in the comics. As a young child it was difficult to understand. With the *Batman* (1966) live action show, the *Super Friends* (1973) cartoon, and even appearances on *Scooby-Doo* (1969), Batman had become a child-friendly hero with harmless villains and weakened consequences. But the comics being published told a different story. Beginning in the 1970s, Batman returned to his dark roots, as seen in Batman #232 the introduction of the terrorist Ra's al Gul, and Batman #251, when Joker returned to being a homicidal maniac instead of the prankster of the 1960s. So would Hollywood follow the trends of Neal Adams and Denny O'Neil?

With popularity of Frank Miller's seminal "The Dark Night Returns," the trend was that comic books weren't just for children anymore. The dark nature of Batman would spill over into the movie theaters, but would it still attract children and be a commercial success?

As an eight year old in 1989 I can assure you that the films that followed would only scare me off if made poorly. With more failures than successes this film franchise is still a series of films that I obsess over. The following are my thoughts on the mainstream, feature length films released in the last thirty years.

There is no film more impactful to the superhero genre than Tim Burton's instant classic *Batman*. At the time the genre was stale. Box office failures of the 1980s, the key failure being the dismal *Superman IV: Quest for Peace*, showed that comic book films needed a shot in the arm.

Everything about this film captured the glory of Batman on the silver screen and showed there was a generation of filmgoers hungry for comic book based heroes. With the curious casting of comedic actor Michael Keaton as the lead many weren't sure if the film would be as serious as the comic books of the 1970s and 1980s. They feared a film similar to the campy Batman TV series.

Tim Burton however, drew inspiration from Alan Moore, Frank Miller, and Denny O'Neil to give us the Dark Knight, a tormented hero whose origin stemmed from witnessed a murder in a dark street ally. From the opening frames of this film we were shown a version of Gotham City that was crafted from the dark recesses of Bob Kane's mind, showing us the corruption of a mobster-controlled city.

Minds were put at ease when Batman showed up in the opening scene to violently beat up drug-addled criminals and threaten them with his fearless presence. What came after was a masterpiece of a comic book film. It gave us a Dark Knight origin, thoughtfully portrayed with flashbacks yet it didn't dwell on the past. Many simply give all of the credit of the film's success to the masterful portrayal of the Joker, played by Jack Nicholson. He may have nearly doomed the rest of the franchise forever because of how perfect he played the role.

Michael Keaton played every aspect of Bruce Wayne so well that it was easy to be overlooked, but I'm always impressed with the nuances of his performance given his screen credits before *Batman*. Enticing action sequences accompanied by gleams of humor in this dark world—everything in this film is a triumph! Music choices were incredible as well. A rousing theme by Danny Elfman and a super powered, funk pop sound track by Prince make the movie a feast for the ears as well as the eyes. *Batman* is one of my first loves as a young boy and made me a comic book enthusiast for life. I believe that all comic book movies live in the fearful shadow of *Batman*!

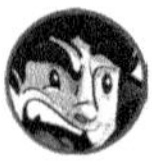

DAN

Batman is one of the most popular superheroes in the DC universe. Many movies, both live action and animated, as well as TV shows have been made about the character over the years, and it's obvious as to why. A superhero who has no superpowers but goes out and fights the bad guys because it's the right thing to do - what's not to love? The guy's pretty darn good at it too; plus he has the coolest toys ever. As you can imagine, with so many interpretations there are a couple of good live action Batman movies and a couple not so good.

To be honest, Keaton's Batman is hard to judge. To start, I felt that Keaton's Bruce Wayne was pretty bland and just didn't feel as powerful of a figure as I believe Bruce Wayne to be. My big thing though is that I don't know if I didn't like Keaton's Batman because of the way he played him or if I didn't like him because of the movement restrictions of the Batsuit. While it has been reported that different suits, capes, and heads were created at a cost of $250,000, the suit seemed to cause Keaton to move around like Darth Vader, not an agile superhero, which made the fight scenes very lackluster.

Batman, as a whole, was alright but would have been much better with a more functional, less restrictive Batsuit—plus the use of more weapons and gadgets would have been cooler than just grappling hooks. It's worth a note that Jack Nicholson's performance as the Joker in *Batman* was very well done. I enjoyed seeing a version of the Joker that began somewhat sane and evolved into the more maniacal Joker

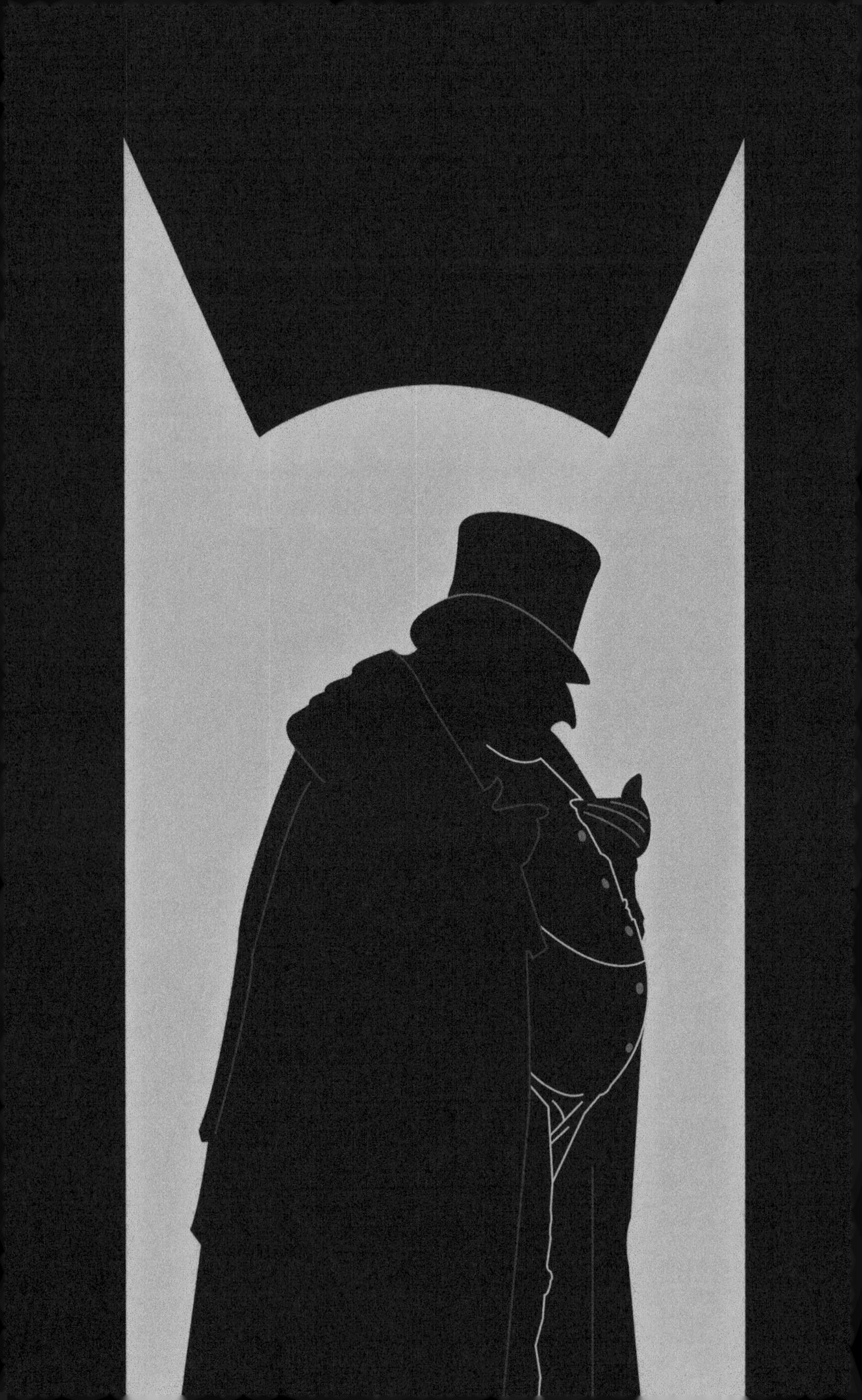

BATMAN RETURNS

 BENNY

This brings us to *Batman Returns*, the first in a series of
Batman movies that fail to maintain a numbering scheme.
This was also the only true sequel that felt in line with the
original movie, due to it being directed by Tim Burton. This
also maintained Tim Burton's insistence that he could tell a
better story if not restricted by the comic book world. He even
started the movie by adding an off-the-wall origin concept
for the Penguin. Instead of being a criminal making his way up
in the crime world, he was a child with fin-like hands being
abandoned by his parents. He was then raised by penguins.

Catwoman got a similar treatment with her being a secretary
that learned too much information; something that gets used
again in the Halle Berry movie that came out almost ten years
later. Catwoman was also placed into a stitched together
outfit instead of being the jewel thief in spandex we had come
to expect. She had more than a few scenes that were chalked
up to an odd fetish Tim Burton had. Being the first film to
feature two villains and two plots also created a series of
problems for the flow of the film.

It felt like two movies smashed into one to create a weird,
stuttering mishmash of a movie. The film as a whole feels
like someone just let Tim Burton have his fun on the second
movie, and that there were no checks and balances. This
might actually be the case because Tim Burton has gone on
record stating that he didn't want to come back for a sequel
unless it offered something new and exciting. I mean, if I had

a world famous director on board that really didn't even want to do it, I would let him do whatever he wanted.

The man on the top of the DC movies train at the time was more concerned with merchandising and toys than making a solid movie at this point. This led to multiple deals, with McDonald's and other major toy manufacturers catching flack for supporting an obviously adult film.

These issues would lead to the departure of Tim Burton. With him gone, we were left with a very solid series of Batman blunders that we all felt the urge to watch. It was like watching someone fail at their job over and over, and you wanted to see the outcome so you could help them back up and tell them: "I told you so. Now get your junk together."

 **JASON**

Batman Returns was one of the most highly anticipated sequels of comic book films yet it proved a failure to live up to the excitement surrounding it. This would be a theme of many comic book films in the exploration of the genre. With key members returning to the production, such as visionary director Tim Burton, superstar in the making Michael Keaton, and legendary composer Danny Elfman, there was good faith around this production. Sadly, not all was right in Gotham.

One of the biggest failings of this film is the loss of the story's central character. While the film is titled *Batman Returns*, it is the villains that dominate the screen time. This mostly has to do with the overabundance in Batman's rogue gallery. The strength of the first movie centered on the character development of Bruce Wayne against the Joker's own character development, which is an incredible dichotomy.

In this film the audience is presented with *two* villains, leaving the central character of Batman lost in the mix. It doesn't help that the villains were not appealing to a younger audience and, in my opinion, poorly portrayed. Penguin being presented as a deformed person did not make his character more appealing but was much more likely to be considered a misunderstood outcast similar to Burton's *Edward Scissorhands*. Michelle Pfeiffer's Catwoman, while looking very impressive, is a somewhat shallow take with her "nine lives." The fact the movie uses so much sexual innuendo with her character as well as Penguin's is astonishing for a movie with a family demographic.

With this return to Gotham City, Tim Burton was allowed substantial creative control so his artistry was dialed up to a higher notch than the previous film. This film felt less true to the comic books and more of a creature of Burton's imagination. This is especially true with the circus freaks in Penguin's gang and the comical use of penguins with rockets on their backs.

The end result is a disappointing return and the beginning of a difficult journey to make Batman films triumphant within the superhero genre.

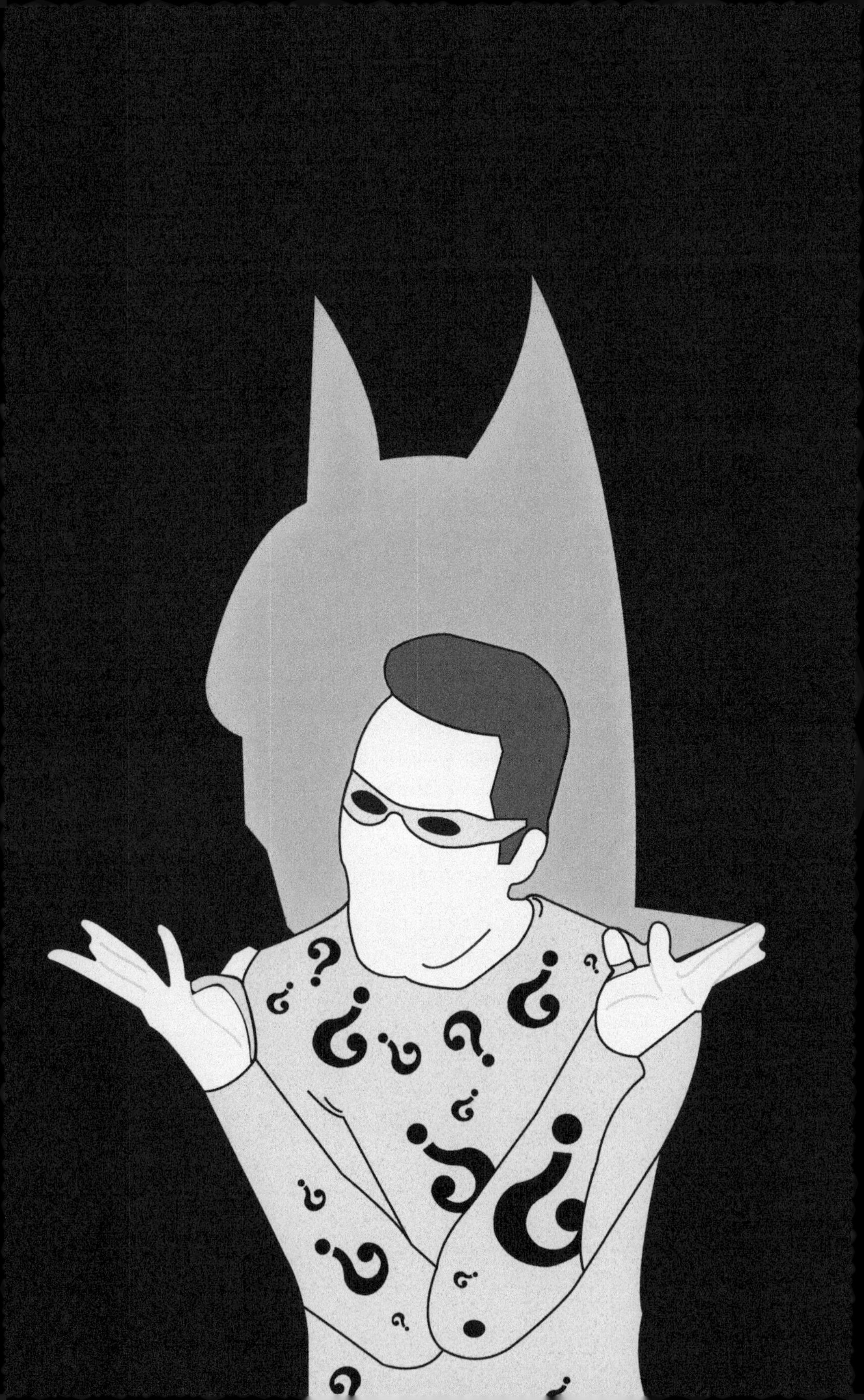

BATMAN FOREVER AND EVER AND EVER

 **BENNY**

Batman Forever continued the trend of failing to properly number the movies. As a child, this was my dream movie: it was going to bring us Robin! (Keep in mind THAT I was a child at the time, and this was a cotton candy-style movie.) It was flashy, colorful and full of wit and humor. This was a stark contrast against the Tim Burton movies which went the dark-and-gloomy yet witty route.

Batman Forever played on my adolescent mind like candy sprinkled on ice cream. The problem is that watching it as an adult shows it's as about as shallow as candy sprinkled on ice cream. It also feels like I got sick from how sweet the film comes across. The colors, tones and attitude are completely opposite from the original two Batman films, something I never noticed as a child. The movie doesn't even feel like it's in the same universe as the original two Batman films. Originally, the film did have a darker cut, bringing the film to a length of two hours and forty minutes. But to keep with the new lighter, cheerier tone, they cut out most of the darker scenes.

Regardless of the original intention of this film, it was just the beginning of the downward spiral: one that would be about toys and merchandising lines and less about great story telling.

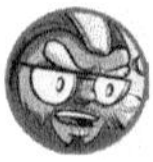

JASON

Batman Forever witnessed a massive turnover in this franchise as far as production was concerned. With Tim Burton spurning the franchise for more personal films, he took on the role of a producer in name only. Joel Schumacher, a director known for taking on darker material such as *The Lost Boys* and *Falling Down*, seemed like a great fit for these stories.

The opening of *Batman Forever* gives the viewer a promising new Batman in the form of Val Kilmer, who is naturally a better choice than Michael Keaton given his dark and mysterious take on the character. Throughout the film he captures the brooding essence of the dual identities and gives what I feel is an honest performance. The movie still seems like his story focusing on his past, grappling with what is happening to Dick Grayson, and struggling with his love life with Dr. Chase Meridian.

While Batman was lost in the shuffle of all of the villains in *Batman Returns* the first half of this film strikes the balance of presenting two new villains, Two-Face and the Riddler. It still manages to tell Bruce Wayne's story, something the comic does so very well. But what about these two villains? Two-Face, played by Tommy Lee Jones, is very campy. A flashback to his origin story is incuded though it is more tragic and serious in the comic. Not much else beyond that is faithful to Two-Face's comic book character; awful make-up and costuming make him a very laughable homicidal threat that seems fairly incompetent at threatening Batman.

One of the most awful aspects of this film is Jim Carrey's Riddler, the least comical villain role. The amount of times he uses his notable physical comedy skills, mastery of overplaying one-liners, and twirling his cane is agonizingly redundant. While there is great production value in this film, Schumacher shows a fondness of bright neon colors throughout the film. He does manage however to show flashes of the Burton style in all things Batman. It's somewhat of an off-putting contrast that he fully embraced in his follow up film.

The bottom line is this is a terrible plot that isn't very reasonable at all. It falls prey to a particular scene in which the villains have nearly killed Bruce Wayne but then let him live for no discernable reason, despite the fact that they have been trying to kill him the whole movie. I found myself enjoying the build-up but by the third reel it falls to shambles. All in all this film is not a complete disaster but it is still greatly removed from the greatness of *Batman.*

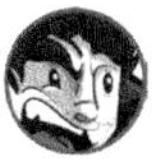

DAN

Val Kilmer kept with the theme of a bland Bruce Wayne—unfortunately—but redeemed himself a little with his Batman. An upgraded and more maneuverable Batsuit, better fights, and a greater variety of gadgets were good improvements from the previous Batman movies.

When watching *Batman Forever*, I began to notice a theme in all these films. While the Batman character was hit-and-miss, the villains were very well acted. While some villain interpretations may not have been as accurate as the comics, the actors themselves did excellent jobs in creating some memorable characters.

Jim Carrey, for example, did a fantastic job at playing the eccentric Riddler, making him smart but also a bit odd. His variety of costumes was also great even if they were designed with very bright neon colors. In fact, the *Batman Forever* film was a lot lighter and brighter in the color scheme, making the creation of toys to support and promote the movie a lot more interesting.

This approach worked very well for the Riddler but kind of diminished the character of Harvey Dent aka Two-Face. The bright colors used didn't make you as afraid of his face as they should have. Instead, the character just seemed way too happy and giggly, not the darker more sadistic Harvey I know. The addition of Robin to the Batman movie franchise was a great choice. It gave viewers someone more light-hearted than Batman to love and opened so many possibilities for sequels that it certainly helped the franchise.

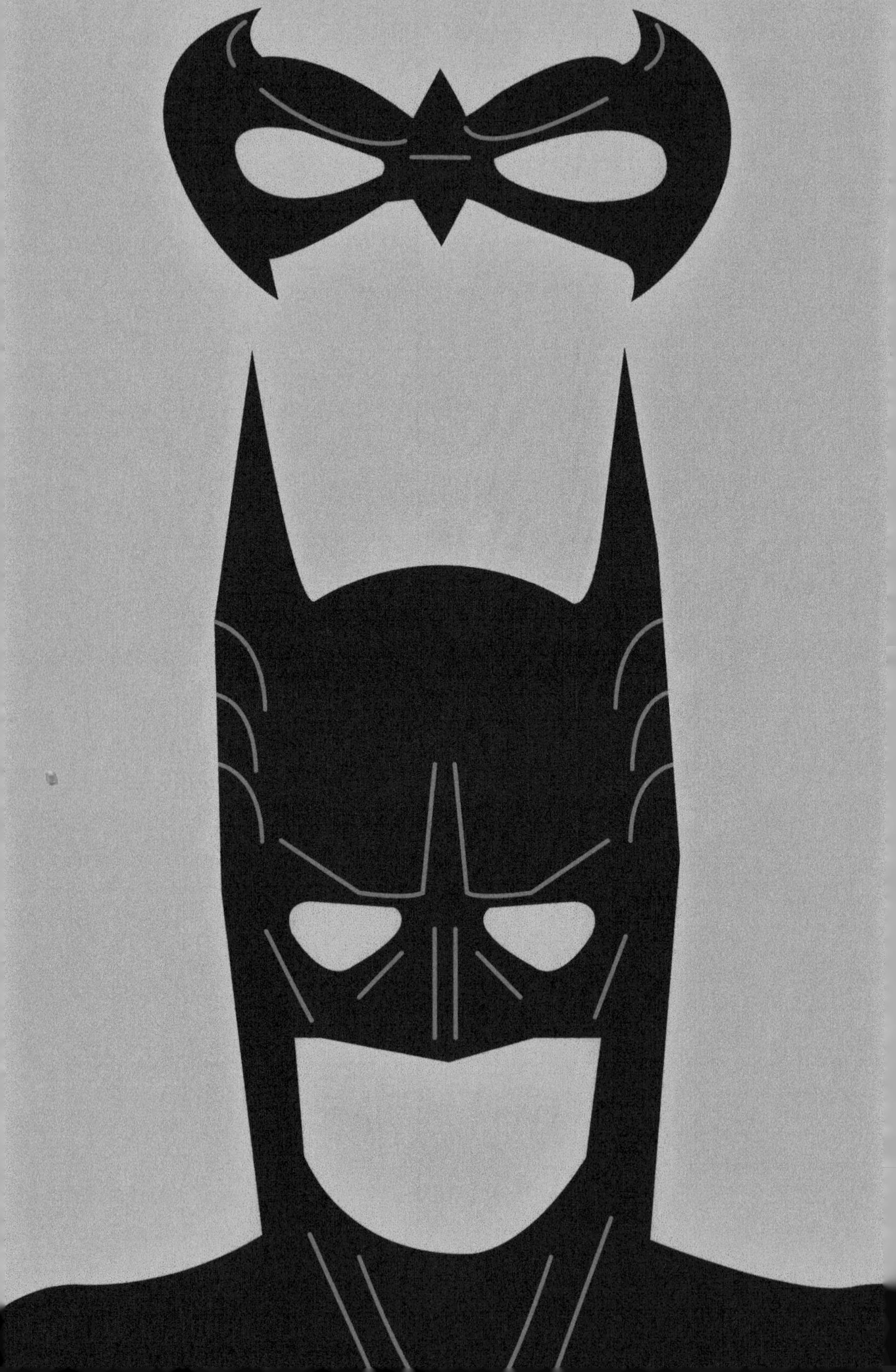

BAT NIPPLES

 **BENNY**

It wasn't until the infamous Bat Nipples and Bat Credit Card that things for Batman truly began to fall back towards the campy nature of the original 1960's series. This was the fourth movie in the franchise: *Batman and Robin*. As we all know, George Clooney was brought in to play Batman. The problem with that is the fact that many amazing actors typically play themselves, and this was what Clooney did. He played his lines with a stiff cornball delivery along with his "Clooney smile" every chance he got.

The movie also carried on with the neon tones and colors: more jokes and humor than any Batman film before it. The icing on the cake: it aimed at selling more toys than ever before. Warner Bros. was really looking for a family friendly film. Joel Schumacher went on record stating that their goal was a much less tortured Batman and a more heroic Batman. There are countless other things that went wrong from here, but luckily this sealed the whole Batman franchise for eight years.

 **JASON**

It's the time we in which we fell to the lowest of lows, the darkest recesses of the Batman franchise. I present to you: *Batman and Robin.* With Joel Schumacher fully at the helm, his vision of making a big budget Batman TV show was realized. *If that is what he was going for I have to tip my hat; he did it.*

With a script by Akiva Goldsman, who would eventually go on to pen Oscar-winning *A Beautiful Mind,* I am flabbergasted that he was ever able to find gainful employment after penning this stinker. Though maybe I should be impressed with the amount of one-liner "freeze" puns he crafted for Arnold Schwarzenegger's Mr. Freeze.

This film reveals itself to be a full admonishment of the comic book genre by Hollywood. It's a film that shows that they just don't understand the importance of comic books on the American mythos. Instead, it is treated as juvenile fantasy that can only entertain, not challenge our understanding of the human condition. George Clooney, the new "it" actor, played Bruce Wayne. He literally bobbed his head and smiled in every scene in which he played Bruce Wayne. Gone is the grim man who lost his family, who has real issues to work through. Clooney, who went on to win an Oscar for his dramatic work in *Syriana*, barely even tries to act in this film.

Uma Thurman's performance as Poison Ivy leaves me breathless. Yes, I couldn't believe what I was seeing. What was she doing? Maybe she wasn't given much to work with in the script but this is her campiest performance—maybe topped by the atrocious, *The Avengers*, a year later. I don't know exactly what she was channeling in her performance but I have a difficult time believing that she could have been happy with what she was doing.

The insertion of Bane into the film, as a man in a suit all "roided" out on Venom, was laughable. This was a character in the comics that was a true threat to Batman, turned into an awful henchman. Now I will say the art direction and the amount of miniatures used in this movie is impressive, but my goodness how many neon colors were used in this film? Please find me a Batman comic where these colors ever existed. Neon green chains? Neon pink graffiti?

Even Mr. Freeze's mouth glowed neon blue. Fans have decried the costume choices for years but it's worth mentioning that in the final scene the three heroes actually change into new suits that have silver highlights! I can just imagine a scene cut from the film in which Batman thought they should stop by the Batcave so they could coordinate their costumes to fight Mr. Freeze. It is no wonder that the Batman franchise was put into deep freeze for nearly a decade. Avoid *Batman and Robin* for it is the harbinger of your doom!

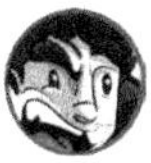

DAN

With the movie *Batman and Robin*, George Clooney played Bruce Wayne/Batman. We were lucky to get the same Robin, played by Dick Grayson, as he did a great job in the *Batman Forever* film. George Clooney was the Batman that opened my eyes to how important a voice change can be. Clooney acted and sounded the same for both Bruce Wayne and Batman; he just wore different suits. It was unfortunate that he didn't change his voice at all, which made it hard to believe that people wouldn't know Batman to be Bruce Wayne. Though it should be noted that Clooney played a fantastic Bruce Wayne as he fits that role so well...but that, in turn, made him a mediocre Batman.

There were some odd choices with costumes in *Batman and Robin*, most notable being the nipples on the armor, which just look straight-up weird. The best part of this Batman film was that the fight scenes and gadgets had improved so much that you could really get into some of those fights. I enjoyed the Bane character in this Batman movie. The use of his venom and its effects on his body were just as I'd imagine: obscure bulging as his body changed and muscles growing until the scrawny guy became a hulk of a man. Mr. Freeze, however, felt out of place and rather dull, not adding much to the movie and—despite being the one of the main villains—just wasn't very memorable. *Batman and Robin* didn't help the franchise much, likely why it was the last Batman movie until the *Dark Knight* Trilogy. Even a Bat credit card can't buy you a good film it seems! At the end of the day, it's worth watching. Just don't get your hopes up too much.

BATMAN BEGINS (AGAIN)

 *BENNY*

A darker-toned Batman film with more humanity injected in than any previous Batman movie. What this brought to the table was the idea of Batman in the real world: not an over the top billionaire with far too much money and toys fighting against impossible villains. No, this was to be the true to life story of Batman. They wanted people to care about Batman and Bruce Wayne. The reason this was such a problem is, as we've said earlier, the Batman films had become about the villains and how Batman reacted to them. This was a trend started back with the Joker and never truly ended.

When Christian Bale came on to play the role, he stated that he felt Batman was an underused character in the previous films. This is what I feel really helped *Batman Begins* do well. It was the first film to truly focus on Batman and give the fans what they wanted. No longer were we doing Batman in Las Vegas with his flashy colors. We had a properly dark and moody Batman. This kicked off the idea that superhero movies could have an edge. They didn't all need to be for children. They could be something adults enjoyed also. It not only influenced future superhero films, but influenced a number of other films.

It was the beginning of darker genre films that retold backstories, or rebooted them entirely in some cases. Now, it's commonplace for a film studio to call for a reboot and try again, but before this it was unheard of: you didn't do this.

 **JASON**

Warner Brothers, after seeing the success of the box office power house *Spider-Man*, knew they would have to re-start their franchises. They handed over creative control to an up-and-coming director named Christopher Nolan, who had independent film success with the incredible crime noir, *Momento*. Nolan directed a great film that attempts to change the game and nature of the Batman franchise and, in my opinion, did all he could to gain back the good will of comic book fans while not being derivative of the Tim Burton films.

The approach to the filmmaking simply asks, "what if Batman were real?" Nolan did his best to ground the film in reality, beginning with the strong casting of Christian Bale, who gives the audience a stellar young Batman. The film pulls from the lore of famous Batman stories, such as *Batman: Year One* and *Batman: Tales of the Demon*. And a lot of credit should be given to David Goyer for taking a serious approach to constructing the script. While Christian Bale is not the "world's greatest detective" in this particular story, the goal was to realistically look at what it would take for a man to become a fearsome vigilante.

When Christian Bale transforms into Batman it is a delight to see him play a character very different from his alter ego, Bruce Wayne. The character had indeed come a long way from the campy performances of the 1990s. The film rang true to the comic book mythos in the portrayal of the mysterious League of Assassins and Bruce Wayne's breaking away from this "cult" to become his own hero. It's a great story that shows a lot of character development in a time in which films tended to shy away from that. In the end, we can see the good-hearted man that Bruce Wayne is as he refuses to become a killer to enact his vengeance. One of my problems with this film is the filming of the combat sequences.

In 2002 the seminal film, *The Bourne Identity*, was released. For this film, audiences were treated to seeing Hollywood actors performing their own fight scenes with modern fighting styles. In order to achieve this the camera is placed closer to the action to envelop you within it and cover up the limited capabilities of the star performer. However, this diverts from the graceful combat choreography that had been utilized in movies such as *The Matrix, Star Wars: The Phantom Menace,* and *Crouching Tiger, Hidden Dragon. Batman Begins* revels in this use of the "Bourne-Style" videography and, in accordance with my tastes, I would rather view the choreography from a distance. It is a trend that is used in films today that I have hoped would end sooner rather than later.

Despite this small hang up the big budget effects, superb art direction, and beautiful photography by Wally Pfister makes *Batman Begins* the film that gave comic book fans what they wanted while leaving them hungry for a future where Batman would evolve into the hero that Gotham City deserved.

THE ONE WITH THE LEGENDARY JOKER PERFORMANCE

 **BENNY**

The success of *Batman Begins* led to entirely new Batman lines of movies and merchandising. It also revived the dormant Batman film franchise by bringing three hundred and seventy-four million dollars in the box office. *The Dark Knight* took the ideas of a realistic world, more human approach to the franchise, and threw in one of Batman's greatest villains: the Joker. Since the original movie was all about Batman, Nolan decided to focus on the Joker, using a lot of the Jokers most notable appearances for inspiration. But Heath Ledger's portrayal of the character is what sold it. It created a dark, complex and unforgettable package for Batman fans to enjoy.

The film is an interesting portrayal of war on terror because when you take a character like the Joker and put him into a real world environment, then that's exactly what he is: a terrorist. Batman wages his war on terror with the aid of Harvey Dent until Dent is changed into the enemy. The whole idea is that having a war on terror breeds more terror. Our white knight is seduced into a world of evil by the actions of the Joker (which is our anarchy).

Before the film's release, Heath Ledger—the actor playing the Joker—passed away. He had a number of health issues, and there were a number of prescription drugs in his system. A popular theory at the time of the movie's release was that playing the Joker took a toll on Ledger's mental well-being, though no evidence was ever presented to fully support this claim. The film brought in over one billion dollars while in the box office, making it the highest grossing Batman film at this time. That is, until the last Batman film in the trilogy.

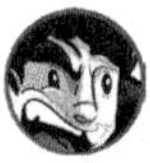

DAN

While this Joker felt different in a way that's hard to explain from the comic book Joker, I thought it was actually for the best. His take on the Joker just felt natural, like he wasn't an actor but the actual Joker himself. It was also nice that his version of the Joker differed from Jack Nicholson's version in the movie, *Batman*, as it removed the direct comparison and allowed you to enjoy each one as their own character.

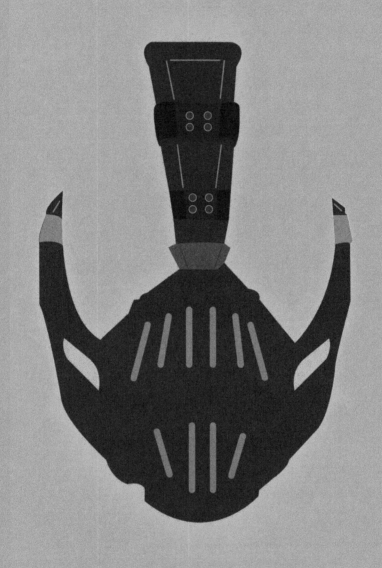

THE DARK KNIGHT RISES

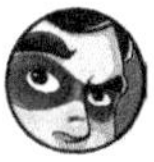

BENNY

There isn't that much to actually say about the last film as we discuss the success of the Batman Film Franchise. At this point it is the highest grossing Batman film, reaching just under one billion one hundred million dollars. The toy sales are a hit, as people have stopped giving Warner Bros. a hard time about having toys for a film children shouldn't see and we are now in a day and age where adult toys exist for collectable purposes. Cinematically, the movie is amazing! Yep, that pretty much sums it up. Plot-holes aside, the movie rocks and I'll fight anyone who says otherwise.

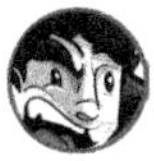

DAN

The third film, *The Dark Knight Rises*, had quite a change in the villain, Bane, played by Tom Hardy. In this version, Bane was no longer powered by venom, had an entirely different origin, different mask, and different demeanor than in the comics. At first, I wasn't a big fan of this new Bane because the differences were so significant. But, as the movie progressed, I began to like this Bane more and more. The change to his character brought to light how different the Batman cinematic universe was from the comics and how it was for the best to remove direct comparisons while keeping the core elements the same. *The Dark Knight* Trilogy was fantastic for the Batman franchise as a whole. Each movie got better and began to solidify this new Batman universe, which brought a lot of people into the comic book world.

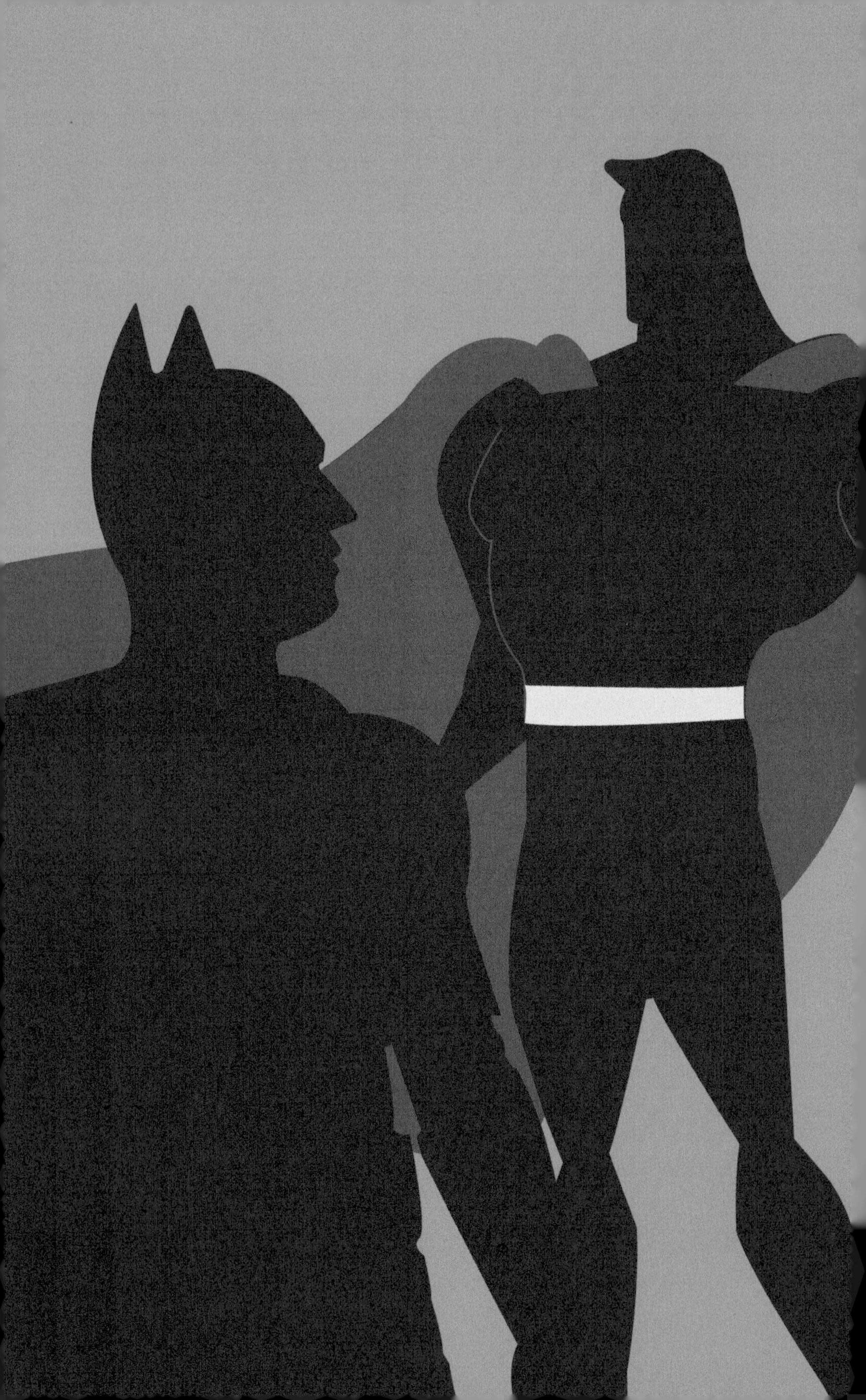

BATMAN v SUPERMAN (AGAIN)

 **BENNY**

Unlike the Superman franchise, which restarted with *Man of Steel*, the Batman franchise came to an end with *The Dark Knight Rises*. Or so we thought. Shortly after announcing there would be a *Man of Steel* sequel, Warner Bros. announced that it would be *Batman v Superman* instead. To the shock of comic books fans all over, our latest Batman film would be a direct battle between Batman and Superman. This would create one of the most dividing superhero movies to date due to its pacing, flow, and character portrayal.

This film also quickly became Warner Bros.'s rush to create an *Avengers* contender by smashing together their own team: the Justice League. We learnt very quickly there would be Wonder Woman in a starring role, and we would also get cameos from various superheroes such as Flash, Aquaman and Cyborg. This is where the problems seemingly stemmed from: the fact the supposed *Man of Steel* sequel had been turned into a way to introduce viewers to the world of what was now being called the DC Extended Universe.

Warner Bros. started an aggressive marketing campaign for the film, reportedly spending over 165 million on making the world aware this movie existed. The reasons for this film are obvious after the success of the Avengers films and the rise of the superhero genre as a whole, but the reception isn't exactly what Warner Bros was hoping for.

Critics and fans were all over the place on opinions, such as hating the new Batman, while many praised him. People disliked the portrayal of Superman within the film, claiming he needed more screen time to tell his story, yet some people wanted less Superman and more of a Batman story. Jesse Eisenberg seemed to be the most dividing element of the film with his portrayal of Lex Luthor coming closer to a mild Joker or a Riddler. Wonder Woman's inclusion in the film, while awesome, felt like an attempt to make the world more aware of her. And hopefully sell toys (something the Batman franchise is already known for trying).

The film quickly settled on a 29% on Rotten Tomatos and a 44% on Metacritic. This states just how dividing the film really is, and it's difficult to officially state that it is better or worse than the reception for *Man of Steel*.

 **JASON**

Finally the showdown all comic fans have waited for *Superman vs. Batman: Dawn of Justice* (2016) is the beginning of what will be considered the DC Cinematic Universe. Warner Brothers realizing the potential of crossing other DC franchises into one movie might be profitable as what Marvel Studios has accomplished. So did this live up to the hype stemming from years of dreaming about seeing both Superman and Batman in the same film? I'm afraid not. This over-bloated, drivel-packed and angst-filled film is a genuine disappointment.

So what is so wrong?

While this film is mostly a sequel to Zack Snyder's *Man of Steel* the film begins with Batman's origin story and leading into an opening segment that is a repeat of the end of the last film from a different point of view. Already the filmmakers are retreading past films, though trying to build the case for Batman to hate Superman. From here on out we are bombarded with several scenes where people talk at each other in meaningless conversations that do not teach us anything new about our returning characters. In eighteen months the people of Earth still seem to be fearful of Superman, Superman doesn't care for Earth all too much, and apparently Lois Lane and Superman are in love, though it would have been nice to see that love story develop at some point.

The characterization of Superman from the previous film is a gigantic disappointment that shows screenwriters do not get that Superman needs to be heroic and inspiring. Instead he is an emotionless alien that cares for no one but those he is personally attached to. This lack of character development makes for a very unemotional ending of the film when Superman sacrifices himself to defeat the giant Doomsday/General Zod hybrid monster. While that moment taken from the famous *Superman* #75 was devastating to comic readers feels like a "so what" moment, and is not a great plot point to build a franchise of the Justice League from.

On top of it all we have Jesse Eisenberg's Alexander Luthor who is a quirkily performed comic villain that is a complete hindrance to the film. This character seems like an insane villain from Batman's rogues gallery of mentally disturbed humans, instead of the criminal mastermind that he should be. This characterization is shameful considering the serious tone of the whole film. So what of the great climactic battle of Superman and Batman? While great efforts were made to give Batman the look of Frank Miller's Batman from *Dark Knight Returns* they seemed to avoid any of the other great moments from that battle.

In the end Batman spares Superman's life and they become "friends" because Batman realizes that their mothers both have the same first name . . . Martha. Really? That's the common ground they reach to become "super friends?" Poor screenwriting by David Goyer is everywhere in this film but that moment is the slap in the face to the audience. The litany of comic sins are too much for me to bear and this film will remain one of the largest squandered opportunities in comic book film history.

The story of Batman in comic book film history is one of constant disappointment for me. What makes him a great hero is long forgotten to cinema and they simply need to get back to his roots. While *Batman Begins* is the last great Batman film, so much has been lost since then. The idea that a hero can't simply be a hero for the sake of goodwill towards man has in recent years been challenged in the medium of film and in comics and is a trend that needs to be changed for this genre to continue to thrive. However with the Justice League franchise full steam ahead I do not foresee a change in sight that will get me behind this character again. In the end I'll continue to watch *Batman* with the same childhood joy that I had back in 1989.

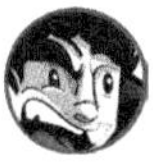

DAN

Batman v Superman: Dawn of Justice was, unfortunately, an example of how not to promote a film within a superhero franchise. The approach to the movie's marketing was off the mark of what viewers would expect to see—viewers that pay good money to be surprised and pleased.

Before the film even came out, my gut-feeling was that the majority of trailers were unnecessarily spoiling some big moments in the movie. This was accompanied by announcements for future films, which simply gave this movie a sort of predictability in how the story would unfold and, due to the already planned future, events with certain characters. After seeing the movie, I learned that my suspicion that there were too many spoilers in the trailers was true. Many big moments could have been so much bigger and more exciting if I didn't already know it was going to happen from watching the trailers.

Another problem was that combining these two major superheroes into a single plot seemed to take away from the story itself. The characters' stories were so brief you barely had time to get into them and, because of this, you were often just waiting for the action to start. The entire first half of the movie felt choppy and somewhat confusing to follow. Maybe it's because I knew about the future films to follow, but it felt like it wasn't really a stand-alone movie and was simply a setup for the future movies already promised. I'm not sure that it's wise to be cautious about being excited for a movie based off the trailers because the trailers are designed to simply get me into the film and may (and often do) include a lot of the good parts of the movie.

I think this would have been much better if it has been developed and released as a TV miniseries to prep for the upcoming Justice League movie that they announced or at the very least a two-part movie, which has been a common trend in the movie business nowadays. This approach would have provided the opportunity to deliver an actual in-depth story for both characters that could have put more meaning, understanding, and excitement into the Batman and Superman encounters, both the conversations and battles. I will say that the action in the fighting was pretty cool, but the battles always felt rather one-sided. The fights and the special effects were well done and gave the movie a hint of epicness, which is what we all want to see.

I also want to include that the actors and actresses played their characters well and the main problems I found with them derived mainly from the script or the directing. While *Batman v. Superman: Dawn of Justice* is a movie worth seeing once, especially with other related movies coming our way in the next few years, but you probably won't want to see it again.

Which is a drag given that sometimes the best thing about a great superhero movie is watching it again and again!

A FINAL LOOK BEHIND THE COWL

 **BENNY**

Just like with Superman, we've got very differing opinions on the Batman movies.

In the end, Batman is just as dividing as Superman and I feel the reason for this is how iconic these two characters are. They have been around for over 75 years at this point, and we have multiple versions and takes on each of these characters. Arguably, the symbol of Superman is more recognizable than anything else in the world. Situations like this create a certain level of expectations when movies are made, and the fans all want their versions of their favorite superheroes. No Superman or Batman movie is so horrendous that it should be burned forever, as there is someone out there that enjoys that particular portrayal of the characters.

This is why they are so dividing, unlike many of the Marvel characters we will explore soon, people know Superman and Batman and know what they want from those movies. Marvel managed to get away with telling stories that only true comic book fans could question, and because of this many were able to view those movies with fresh eyes.

But now that we have looked at two of the most dividing franchises in the superhero genre, it's time to look at one of the mostly accepted franchises, even if it started with nothing more than failure.

CHAPTER 3:

MARVEL
BEFORE IT WAS
MARVEL

 **JASON**

Marvel comics are near and dear to me now more than ever. While it was DC Comics movies that captured my imagination as a child it is now the Marvel licensed films that keep me inspired as a filmgoer. Growing up it seemed impossible to do any of the Marvel characters justice on screen. Maybe it was because their stories were larger than life or that the effects needed to create these films simply weren't available. But we never stopped imagining what these films would be like on the silver screen. The road to making Marvel films great has been a long one. They have hit very low points and experience many bumps on the road before reaching a very powerful triumph in the end, which brings us to today. It seems now Marvel can do no wrong when you look at the box office results of these movies. But box office success doesn't prove that a movie is faithful to the comics.

Before we get to our analysis, let's examine some of the lesser known movies that built the foundation of success.

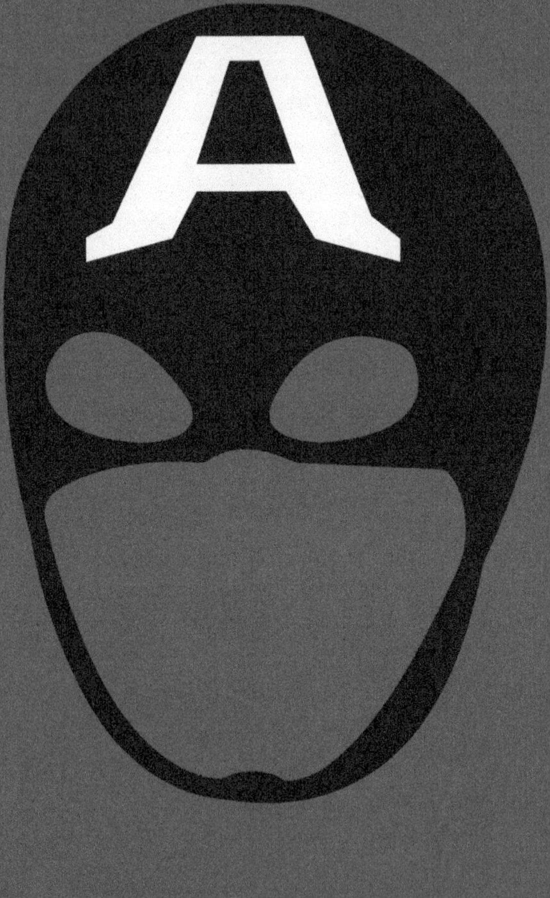
A

CAPTAIN AMERICA

The first cinematic film to feature a Marvel character was *Captain America*, released by independent film production studio, Republic Pictures, on February 5, 1944. The serial included 15 episodes, totaling 243 minutes of black and white action-packed drama. It would be Republic's last superhero serial, in fact, one of the last by any studio at the time.

You'd be hard-pressed to find similarities between the 1944 adaptation of Captain America and the original Timely Comics (known today as Marvel Comics) character. Republic Pictures completely abandoned the basic comic book premise portraying Captain America, instead as District Attorney Grant Gardner who wields a regular, plain gun. The story includes no Army setting, no Super Soldier Serum, no shield, no Nazis, and no sidekick Bucky.

Timely Comics wasn't happy with replacing Steve Rogers with DA Grant Gardner and making other fundamental changes. While they let their views be known, Republic Pictures stuck with their version pointing out that any production changes would be costly and the studio had no contractual obligation to keep with the original storyline. Some believe the script was written for an entirely different superhero and that it was decided later on to change this character to become Captain America. Others think the story was modified to be more entertaining for the audience, who was dealing with real war, real soldiers fighting, and real Nazis at the time.

Captain America was the most expensive serial Republic Pictures had created, costing $220,000. While the series had a different character, different backstory, and different villains, it offered suspense and special effects, including guillotines and exploding cars. Grant Gardner was a guy who knew how to punch, use a gun, and wear a tight suit. The serial offered viewers super-weapon thrills including the "Dynamic Vibrator" and "Electronic Firebolt." The black and white filming meant Captain America's costume colors were grey, white, and dark blue so they could photograph better. There were no wings on his head, but miniature flags were added to his gloves and his belt buckle had a small shield.

There were a few main characters throughout the series including Gail Richards (Gardner's secretary) played by Lorna Gray, Police Commissioner Dryden played by Charles Trowbridge, Mayor Randolph played by Russell Hicks, and Doctor Cyrus Maldor (also known as The Scarab) played by Lionel Atwill. Dick Purcell, who died at age 36 of a heart attack shortly after filming was complete, played Captain America/Grant Gardner. John English and Elmer Clifton directed the serial.

While the dialogue and story might be a bit corny, the shows were filled with suspense and offered entertainment for the audience. Captain America's promotion tagline was all caps and stated: "BLAZING ACROSS THE SCREEN IN A SERIAL OF REAL LIFE ADVENTURES!"

BLADE

Next up is 1998's *Blade*. In a time when comic book-based movies were failing at the box office, *Blade* was in production and about to be released. The original concept began in 1992 when producer Peter Frankfurt contacted Marvel Comics to explore whether any African-American comic heroes existed. They said they had a mid-level comic character called Blade.

Peter Frankfurt worked with (uncredited) producer Michael De Luca, who had an option on Blade for New Line Cinema. The film was conceived to star rapper/actor LL Cool J playing the lead role and be directed by David Fincher, who had just finished *Se7en*. Neither of these players panned out, and the team spent several years looking for the best writer, director, and lead actor.

David Goyer was hired to create the screenplay, delivering a first draft of the script in eight weeks. He had a vision that delivered powerful material that he knew couldn't be made cheaply. He was surprisingly supported with the funding. Wesley Snipes was next identified as the ideal action superstar and brought on for the lead role. It would be years to find the right director for the film, but they found a good fit in Stephen Norrington, director of *Death Machine*. After five years, *Blade* went into production.

Blade was released on August 21, 1998. The character, created by writer Marv Wolfman and artist Gene Colan, was originally introduced in 1972 in Marvel's "The Tomb of Dracula" comic book series and went on to be included in other comics including Nightstalkers and Dr. Strange. Blade was not a highly popular comic book character, and the movie only loosely followed the original story. In the comic, Blade is a tough-talking vampire raised by a vampire hunter, Jamal Afari. He was immune to becoming a vampire and instead was part of a group of vampire hunters who mainly fought Dracula. Blade's enemy was an older, white-haired vampire alchemist, Deacon Frost.

In the film a younger actor, Stephen Dorr, plays Blade's enemy, Deacon Frost. The role was initially offered to Jet Li, but he was committed to the production of *Lethal Weapon 4*. Abraham Whistler served as Blade's mentor in the movie and was played by Kris Kristofferson. As of yet, Whistler hasn't been included in any Marvel Comics. Marc Singer (of *The Beastmaster* series) was the original choice to play Whistler. N'Bushe Wright played Dr. Karen Jenson, Donal Logue played Quinn, and Udo Kier played Gitano Dragonetti, Blade's rival in the vampire world.

With a budget of $45 million, the filming of *Blade* took place from February to June of 1997. Locations were primarily in California including downtown Los Angeles, Long Beach, and Death Valley.

The film offers a highly visual style, extreme camera angles, larger-than-life sets, and an enormous amount of blood. Special effects were present as massive explosions, wirework, and an intense showdown at the vampire temple. However, the real action came from martial arts fighting and action scenes. There were swords, weapons, a flying guillotine, and stylish, choreographed violence; Wesley Snipes said the role was the most physically demanding of his career. The scenes and content were intense and, in some cases, too intense. The studio demanded a scene be excluded, which featured a live vampire baby held inside a jar, as it was too disturbing. In some cases, the digital special effects are seen to be subpar because they weren't yet commonplace and very expensive. In its first viewing, *Blade* was horribly received by the audience, forcing many edits and re-shoots, delaying the release by about one year.

The release of *Blade* helped kick off the Marvel Comics film franchise machine and also started a wave of vampire interest and shows. *Blade* grossed $70 million in the U.S. and $131 million worldwide. The subsequent DVD release was the first to include premium and additional contents, extra features, new scenes, and a director's interview. The movie had two promotional taglines: "The power of an immortal. The soul of a human. The heart of a hero," and "Against an army of immortals, one warrior must draw first blood."

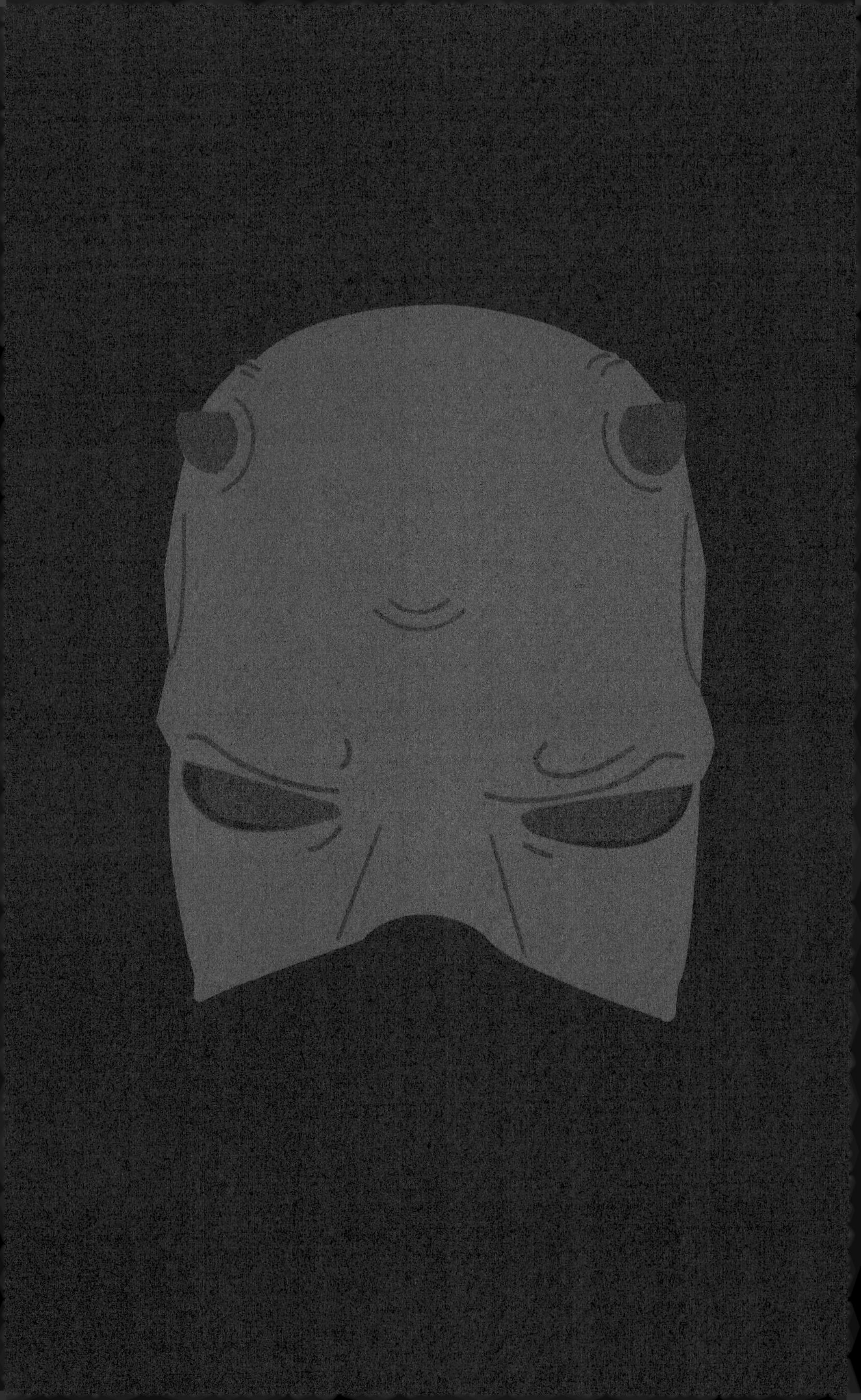

DAREDEVIL

Finally, in the collection of how far we've come, there is Ben's *Daredevil*. Stan Lee and Bill Everett introduced the Daredevil character in 1964, a blind superhero whose remaining senses are ultra-sensitive, including a special type of radar capability. The character was revived when he underwent a reinvention in the 1980s as Marvel Comics' artist/writer Frank Miller adapted Daredevil with darker themes, religious imagery, and a passion for martial arts. The character Elektra, also created by Frank Miller, was introduced shortly after.

Development for a Daredevil film began in 1997 when 20th Century Fox optioned the rights from Marvel Enterprises. In 1998, however, Marvel was nearing bankruptcy and 20th Century Fox allowed the option to expire. After the concept went through various studio negotiation attempts, in 2000 New Regency Enterprises obtained the character rights to produce the film and have 20th Century Fox distribute. Various scripts and screenplays were developed and rewritten over the years, including one by Chris Columbus (writer of *Gremlins* and *The Goonies*), before director and screenplay writer Mark Steven Johnson (writer of *Grumpy Old Men* and *Jack Frost*) joined the production. Johnson delivered a screenplay for production in 2001.

Several actors, including Matt Damon, Colin Farrell, and Vin Diesel, were considered to play the part of Matt Murdock/ Daredevil. In the end, Ben Affleck was brought on for the role. Colin Farrell was, instead, hired to play the part of Bullseye. Ben Affleck claimed that Daredevil was his favorite comic book as a kid, having read every single issue for the part. Penelope Cruz, Natalie Portman, and Katie Holmes were considered for Elektra, but Jennifer Garner secured the role in the end. Michael Clarke Duncan played Kingpin, and Jon Favreau played Franklin "Foggy" Nelson. David Keith played Matt's father, Jack Murdock.

Daredevil was filmed primarily using Los Angeles locations although the story is based around Hell's Kitchen in Manhattan, New York. Matt Murdock's apartment was on South Broadway in L.A., the same as used in the movie, *S.W.A.T.* The Millennium Biltmore Hotel was used for the black and white party, which was also a film location in *Beverly Hills Cop*. The church interior, in Daredevil's opening scene, is in Downtown L.A. and was also used for *Spider-Man 2* and *National Treasure*.

While most of the special effects are not acclaimed, the CGI used for Daredevil's "sonar vision" to visualize Elektra is of particular note. Ben Affleck wore milky blue contact lenses, which made him effectively blind. Digital effects were used to illustrate noise producing sonar waves for the character to "see." Considerable choreography was used, including an extreme sports style known as Parkour that allows for martial art acrobatic skills during fight scenes.

Daredevil is particularly faithful to the comic books, including the addition of supporting cast who play parts in the comics. Minor characters have been named after various Daredevil artists and writers over the years, and the movie includes a cameo by Frank Miller, who plays the "man with pen in head" role—one of Bullseye's victims. The origin and costume of Daredevil are right, with small horns on the cowl and Double D logo. There were minor modifications, however, including making the Kingpin character white in the movie and putting

Elektra in black leather instead of the red satin she often wore in the comics.

The movie released on Valentine's Day, February 14, 2003. With a budget of $78 million, the film managed to gross $179.1 million worldwide, $102.5 in the U.S. alone. It was the second biggest release for the month of February (behind Hannibal) but first place in the opening weekend, grossing $45 million. A director's cut of the movie was released in 2004, R-rated, which added 30 minutes of extra footage and a new subplot.

The movie's promotional tagline was "When justice is blind, it knows no fear."

THE MARVEL CINEMATIC UNIVERSE (AND SONY... AND FOX)

BEHIND THE SCENES: WHAT WAS GOING ON?

 **BENNY**

As Jason just detailed, the problems began way back in the 40s because Timely Comics (Marvel Comics' original name) didn't like the portrayal of the character. Captain America wasn't Steve Rogers frozen in time, or even a war hero. Republic Pictures completely abandoned the basic comic book premise and portrays Captain America as District Attorney Grant Gardner, who wields a regular, plain old gun. The story includes no Army setting, no Super-Soldier serum, no shield, no Nazis, and no sidekick Bucky. This was just the start of problematic productions failing to properly represent their source material.

While I can't find any evidence to support my theory, the fact that Marvel avoided making movies for forty-some years basically says they were scared to work with the movie companies. Eventually, they decided to try again with the character *Howard the Duck* in 1986 and *The Punisher* in 1989. This was most likely in response to the seeming success of *Superman* and *Batman*, but, as we know, neither movie proved to be a success. Marvel was also still trying to sell the rights to their characters, allowing movie studios to do whatever they wanted.

Originally they had a plan to launch a series of Marvel themed restaurants called Marvel Mania, but the first one closed up within the first year. They also looked into launching new trading cards and a CD-ROM line. Neither of these ideas even got off the ground. They instead began selling licensing rights to all of their most popular properties. The problem was that with this deal Marvel would make a good chunk of money up front, but practically nothing on the backend. An example was the first modern Marvel movie, *Blade*: it grossed $70 million but Marvel only pocketed something in the area of $25,000. Fox then got the rights to the X-Men, basically launching the modern era of superhero movies following the success of *Blade* and the infamous Sam Raimi *Spider-Man* trilogy.

Their properties took off to great success, but Marvel was still barely making any money from it. A talent agent made a pitch to Marvel: to produce these movies in house, keeping creative control and all the money on the backend for themselves.

They were iffy on the idea, but in 2005 they signed a deal to give it a shot. Since they were still recovering from bankruptcy, they had to put something on the line in order to receive the amount of money they needed to get things started. They had already given up the X-Men and Spider-Man, along with a bunch of other characters. So they offered up the rest of their characters as collateral: Captain America, The Avengers, Nick Fury, Black Panther, Ant-Man, Cloak and Dagger, Doctor Strange, Hawkeye, Power Pack and Shang-Chi. If their movies bombed, they would have lost the rights to everything and the Marvel Cinematic Universe would have never existed.

History speaks for itself, and the original *Iron Man* kicked off as one of the highest grossing films ever. Marvel was set to eventually sell the franchise to Disney. But there's a reason they were able to make Iron Man so good. The X-men franchise and Spider-Man franchise set them up in incredible ways. They knew what would work, what wouldn't work, and what the fans really wanted.

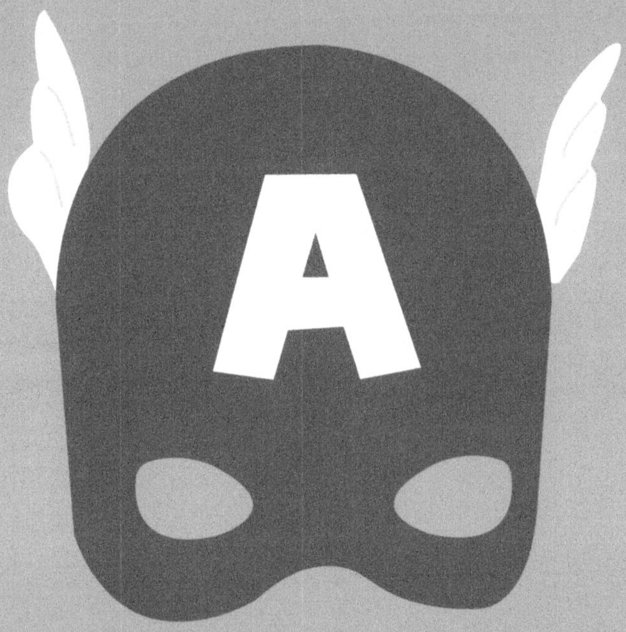
A

Captain America (Again)

 BENNY

This became the situation with *Captain America*. Not the one you are probably familiar with, but the original 1990 version of the character. The film rights bounced around and the budget never seemed to exist. Rather large notable, changes took place as well, such as making Red Skull an Italian fascist and not a Nazi, no Bucky, and randomly moving Cap's hometown to California. The decisions didn't seem to make any sense at all and were arbitrary. Cap acted out of character in very notable ways, such as stealing cars and decapitating villains. While I'm aware the decapitation was the villain's own mistake for getting in the way of the shield, it still was very out of character for Captain America.

Things only went downhill from here as the film rights for the Fantastic Four were also purchased and the movie was so bad it was never officially released. This movie actually ran its trailers in movie theaters and was all set for an official release. Then, it magically vanished. There aren't any confirmed stories behind its failure to launch, but there are a couple of running theories. One theory is that the film was made solely to hold the rights to the Fantastic Four with no intention of actually releasing it. The other theory is that just before it was to be released, Marvel paid to have the film destroyed in an attempt to preserve their brand. The concern was that there was going to be another FF movie coming out shortly after this one, and with THIS being so low budget THAT no one would want to see the second one.

 **JASON**

This film is borderline unwatchable and it's hard to believe that this could even compete with contemporary comic book films such as *Batman* or *Dick Tracy*. While this film at least used names such as Steve Rogers and Red Skull, they are simply in name only. The film did its best to portray Project Rebirth, the mythological origin of Steve Rogers that transformed him into Captain America, but it just seems to falter. The casting decision to have a single actor portray Steve Rogers before and after his transformation loses any impact that the moment holds. While this might have come off as a rip off of the television show, *The Incredible Hulk*, Matt Salinger does not show the audience a powerful transformation before and after the key scientific experiment. Captain America is actually not really good at anything in this movie. He loses his first major fights, making him very difficult to be impressed by. Shoddy action sequences and horrible costuming keep this film from being taken seriously.

For some reason the script chose to make Red Skull Italian though thankfully they did not shy away from his association with the Nazi Party; yet he is still a weak villain with paltry motives. One of the most laughable parts of the movie is when Captain America, attached to a missile, flies from Europe to Washington D.C. and then somehow diverts the missile all the way to Alaska in a feat of reality warping physics! This film showed how far behind Marvel was at adapting their comics to compete against the stellar blockbuster films of the 1980s.

S.H.I.E.L.D.

 **JASON**

If there is a low point in our exploration of the comic book genre, *Nick Fury: Agent of S.H.I.E.L.D.* (1998) is indeed scraping the bottom of the barrel. It is somewhat unfair to compare this to Hollywood blockbusters because this was a made for television film which means there is a very limited budget. So how bad is this movie? Staggering. Wretched. Alcoholism inducing. To think David Goyer, who wrote *Blade* in the same year he wrote this, is a shock to the senses. This film has so many laughable moments it's hard to believe that Marvel could ever be taken seriously in film ever again. Having said that, this film at least has nods to what happened in the comics and it seems like David Hasselhof believed he was seriously portraying the great Nick Fury.

However, this film is laughable. It's totally worth seeing for the nearly unwatchable effects of a S.H.I.E.L.D. Heli carrier. The portrayal of Viper is the stuff of B-Movie legend. Sandra Hess gives us an over the top screen villain that is quite memorable and makes so many bad performances look so good. I actually find this horrible performance much better than the version of Viper in *The Wolverine*, so there is something nice to say about it. However, the terrible plot, the awful supporting cast, the ghastly visual effects, and sickening Hasselhof one-liners make this one of the most atrocious comic book films I have ever seen. Marvel films could only go up from here, but that's not saying much. Watch this film for the sheer terror of what might be Marvel's worst hour.

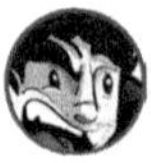

DAN

Just when you thought it couldn't get any worse, the 1998 *Nick Fury: Agent of S.H.I.E.L.D.* was released and put what seemed like the final nail in the coffin. *Nick Fury* starred David Hasselhoff, who liked to chew on cigars more than he liked to smoke them. This film felt like a homemade movie you make for a college class on a tiny budget. The promotional tagline was "The Last Superhero!," which seemed telling. Long story short, this is a movie to avoid and, although it didn't help Marvel's movie reputation at the time, maybe it was part of the path for better things to come.

The first couple of decent Marvel movies to come were *Spider-Man* and *X-Men*. When I was a kid, *Spider-Man* was one of the first superhero films I ever saw - and I can say I really enjoyed it. The movie had a character I could relate to that had super cool and unique powers. While it did have some differences to the comic book character, such as his webs shooting from his wrists and not from the homemade web fluid cartridges, it was still pretty true to the original comics. The first film in the trilogy was fantastic and gave a good look at Spider-Man, Peter Parker, Mary Jane, Goblin—all the main characters in the Spider-Man comics. However, as Marvel created the second and third movie installments, I personally, started to lose some interest.

STARTING TO FIGURE IT OUT (X-MEN)

 **BENNY**

The first film came out in 2000, but that's not when it all started for this franchise. Talks for a film actually began as early as 1984. The film rights rested with a company called Orion Pictures. But they stalled in making the film, so the rights reverted back to Marvel. In 1990, Stan Lee and Chris Claremont started talking with Carolco Pictures to try and get James Cameron as the producer. At this time, Bob Hoskins was being considered for the role of Wolverine and Angela Basset for Storm. It was actually Stan Lee that ruined this film when he got James Cameron interested in producing a Spider-Man film instead. This didn't happen either, but that's a story further in our history. The rights floated around for a bit until FOX had a successful animated show called **X-Men**. Realizing they had a potential goldmine, FOX optioned to buy the rights to the X-Men when Marvel was going through their bankruptcy. What is notable about *X-Men* is the impact this film had.

The first X-Men movie proved that superhero movies could be good again. Many people only remembered the classic Superman from the 70s and the Batman from the 80s. While the 90s did bring us *Blade*, it was the beginning of the CGI era of films, and *X-Men* was the game changer. Before *X-Men*, practical effects had to be used, which for superhero movies made things look clunky and weird at times. Batman's grappling hook and Superman's flight look were made with practical effects, but they never looked legendary or fantastic. They always looked like a guy on strings being pulled around. *Blade* was the beginning of it, but that was still pretty early on, so they weren't completely sure how to use it. They even had a scene near the end that they changed completely because they couldn't get the CGI to look right. When it came to *X-Men*, Bryan Singer wanted to begin diving into the ideas behind CGI by studying two recent CGI-oriented films: *Star Wars Episode I* and *Titanic*. He wanted a mix of practical and CGI effects. They didn't overdo it, and combined with giving the heroes real substance, leading to an amazing climax at the Statue of Liberty, we were shown the fantastic superheroes we were expecting.. *X-Men* showed the world superhero movies were something. You have to enjoy a movie where the biggest complaint was the lack of proper costumes and the use of black leather on everyone. This led to multiple sequels, and we'll get to those in a minute. Next up was the Spider-Man movie.

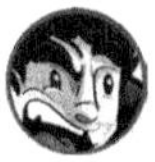

DAN

The X-Men movies kicked off in 2000. These were also films I watched before I became a comic book reader and fanatic and because of this, for me, I kind of miss the impression they made on me before I knew the comics! When I first watched these movies I really enjoyed all the films. They had great action, super cool effects, and so many different types of powers than other movies that focused mainly on a single superhero with limited powers. The X-Men films contained over 10 mutants, each with different and unique powers and personalities. The first time watching these films, before I became a comic book reader, I had no background to work off of so there wasn't much to criticize or be disappointed with. They were simply good fun! This all changed, however, the more I began reading the X-Men stories. Now that I know all that I know, when I re-watch these films I start seeing flaws: incorrect names, different looks than the comics, and sometimes completely different characters entirely—I'm looking at you Deadpool from *Wolverine Origins*! Don't get me wrong, the films are definitely worth watching, but I think with some more serious consideration of the comics and backgrounds, they could've done a better job to really do the X-Men justice.

Success (Spider-Man)

 **BENNY**

After Stan Lee convinced James Cameron to produce a Spider-Man film instead of an X-Men film, it went into development hell. Once Sony Pictures finally picked it up, they completely retooled the script by bringing in their own team. The result was the origin story of Spider-Man, which had never been portrayed on the big screen before. While *X-Men* showed that superhero movies could portray a substantial story and characters, *Spider-Man* showed that if you got the formula correct, it could also be one of the highest grossing films ever. While it has fallen from its high pedestal with more and more movies coming out, at the time this film led to the highest grossing single day of sales.

The film won multiple awards and cemented the idea that a superhero film could not just perform well, but also resonate well with the comic book fans. While it wasn't completely true to the comic book stories and characters, it was the closest the movie going public had received up to this point. We have traveled far from our Californian Captain America and our comically bad, unreleased Fantastic Four film. Sure, with *Spider-Man* we had a horrible costume on the Green Goblin and organic webbing, but we also had Uncle Ben, Aunt May, Harry Osborne and a radioactive spider.

With the success of *X-Men* and the insane performance of *Spider-Man*, Marvel started to realize there was something special with these movies. It was at this moment that a talent agent approached them with the idea of making their own movies.

More and more Marvel themed movies came out to varying degrees of success, but each and every one of them did well in the box office. It was a combination of CGI coming into full swing and the featuring of recognizable characters that many people remember from their childhood. But something else happened during this surge of superhero movies.

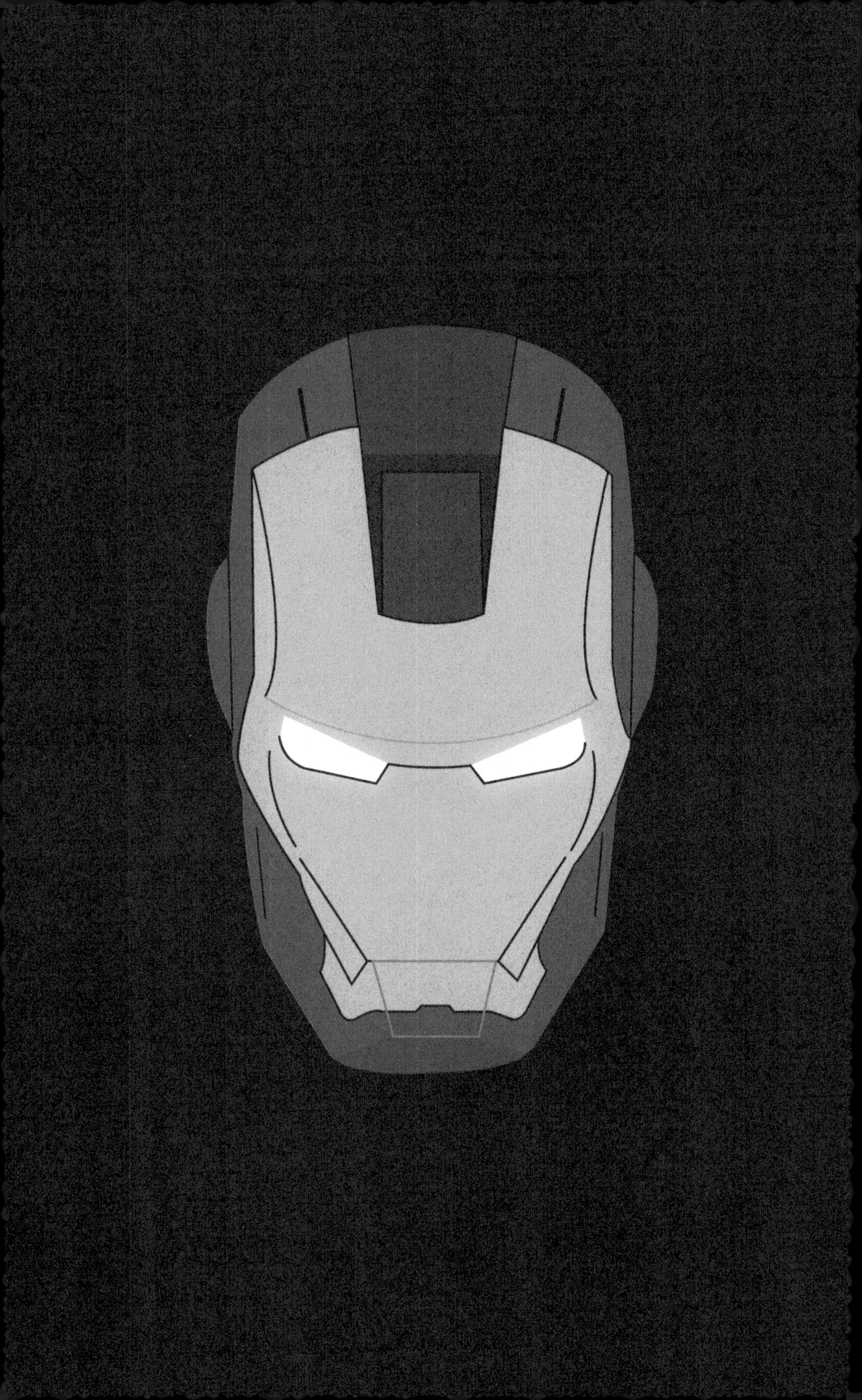

BLOWING THE COMPETITION AWAY (IRON MAN)

 **JASON**

Iron Man is the film where filmgoers were welcomed to the Marvel Age! This is hands down the most significant comic book film of recent history. What Jon Favreau and Marvel Studios put together in this film is indeed a modern movie marvel! What is incredible about this movie is that it takes a comic book character that has more of a cult following and married him to an actor who propelled him to another level. Robert Downey Jr. is Tony Stark; it is just that simple. While Stark can be a little more serious in the comics, Downey Jr. embraced the gearhead persona to such a level that in many ways there is no turning away from this casting. With whizz-bang effects that live up to the art of the comics, it's the humanity of Tony Stark that the audience latches onto. Despite that Tony is a playboy-billionaire-tech-genius that most people couldn't sympathize with, his incredible compassion for humanity allows viewers to believe in heroes. With character flaws galore, he somehow becomes more grounded in a world where the laws of physics are being warped.

The handling of this character is superb and is the benchmark of all comic book films to follow. With an updated origin taken straight from Warren Ellis' phenomenal comic book and art inspired by the uncanny Adi Granov comic book fans couldn't feel more appreciated. Most importantly this film began the art of the "tease," in which new characters and concepts would be introduced without dwelling on them for too long, in the hopes of setting them up for a future film. I can't say enough about this film. Watch *Iron Man* over and over because this is why fans obsess over comic book films!

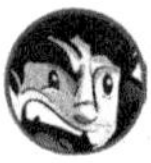

DAN

One of the biggest game changers to the superhero movie world was when Marvel Studios released *Iron Man* in 2008; its first film in the Marvel Cinematic Universe. The movie was fantastic and very accurate to the comics and really revived superhero movies for the entire industry. While the screenplay, special effects, and direction did a fantastic job at introducing the comic book characters, it was really how well the actors played these roles that brought it to life. Robert Downey Jr.'s version of Tony Stark was spot-on and really brought forward a unique personality for a superhero, something I really liked. Another of the big aspects I really liked was how realistic it was. Okay, maybe not "realistic" in the sense that it could happen today, but realistic that, in their universe, it didn't feel out of place or unbelievable. Fantastic. Keeping the rights to their superhero characters in-house, and funding their own movies, Marvel Studios was—at last—really on its way.

Just a month after the Iron Man release, in June 2008, Marvel released *The Incredible Hulk*. While not as good as *Iron Man*, *The Incredible Hulk* was a good movie. The Hulk wasn't your normal superhero, many may not even call him a hero at all. He's a scientist that goes on rampages when he loses his temper, which unleashes strength and power like no one can imagine. These "powers" brought to light that superheroes weren't all good and they definitely weren't perfect but, if given the right help and guidance, they definitely could be great. I thought the graphics were done rather well for the film and while it definitely wasn't the best movie, at least it wasn't *Nick Fury: Agent of S.H.I.E.L.D.*!

 **JASON**

After the smash hit of *Iron Man,* Marvel sought to focus the development of their universe around Tony Stark in *Iron Man 2* (2010). With the full production team back on for this film it would be a great opportunity for Tony Stark to grow as well as introduce more elements of the MCU. While this film is by no means a masterpiece of the comic book film genre, it does the job of being greatly entertaining while adding components to the film franchise. With a bevy of returning characters and the first appearance of Black Widow, played by Scarlett Johanssen, and War Machine, played by Don Cheadle, Marvel showed audiences what they had to look forward to in future films. With S.H.I.E.L.D. beginning to play a bigger role in each Marvel film, it was becoming apparent that they were serious about building their universe in every single film they produced.

While the plot itself wasn't anything new it didn't have to be. The focus was on world building and entertaining the audience at the same time, and they pulled that off. The biggest strength of this film is of course Robert Downey Jr. playing Iron Man. He continued to encompass the character of Tony Stark, as a man who could act witty and still become a righteous hero, as a man who would man up in the face of adversity. Playing hard and working hard are traits that he shows in spades, taking a character that in the comics was not a "best-selling" character and making him best-selling. *Iron Man 2* signaled a great future in comic book films.

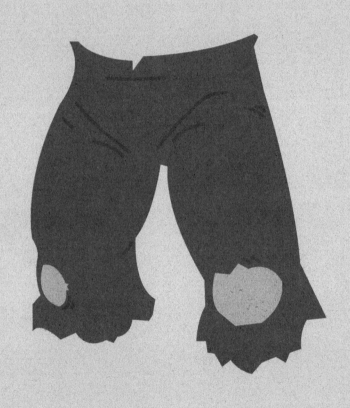

HULK

 **JASON**

With the release of the *Incredible Hulk* (2008) we were going to go back to a Marvel license that had been made into a film by master craftsman, Ang Lee. However, Marvel Studios decided to steer clear of that production as much as they could in order to tie it into their Marvel Cinematic Universe (MCU). So just like in *Iron Man* they brought in top talents within the film industry to bring the Hulk to life. I found this film to be a pale shadow of the previous film and a waste of the talents of Edward Norton, which we later learned had spats with director Louis Leterrier, of the *Transporter* film franchise.

The main production theme to this film was to return to the ideas of the popular television show of the 1970s, in which Dr. Banner was on the run from the United States Government. While this is where the last film left off there was a different tone influenced by the *Bourne Identity* and did not feel like a fresh take on the character. Liv Tyler's portrayal of Betty Ross seemed fairly laughable as she did not exude the intelligence of her character, but she wasn't given much to work with. A painful moment for me in the film is when Bruce Banner's sexual arousal during a moment of intimacy is avoided because he might "Hulk-out." "Hulking out" is not a blood pressure issue; it's about anger and rage.

The filmmakers seemed to show a lack of understanding the character. The special effects in my opinion were nowhere near the technical finesse of Ang Lee's *Hulk* and that was highly disappointing to me as a viewer. However, this film did have a scene with Tony Stark, the first witness of Marvel building their universe. It is apparent that Marvel Studios have nearly abandoned this film in their franchise as they have simply made Hulk a part-time character in the MCU.

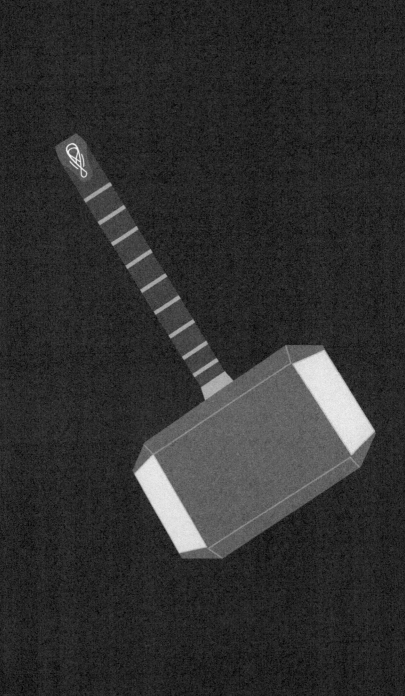

THOR

 **JASON**

One of the biggest challenges in building the MCU came with the out of this world release of *Thor* (2011). So far everything in the MCU was focused on science and heroes who originated on planet Earth. Though the production was handed over to a Shakespearean thespian, in the guise of Kenneth Brannagh, this film turned out to be far from the legendary mythos that took place in the comic books. There was a major deviation from the comics, in which the people of Asgard were from another planet instead of being the Norse gods that they are in the books. To me this is disappointing because it eliminates the idea of magic and faith from the Marvel Universe, an important aspect of the comics.

To me this film falls flat and does not live up to the brilliance of the Thor comics. This likely stems from their decision to deviate from the Thor and Donald Blake dual identity that is prevalent in the Marvel mythos. Odin could have simply cast Thor into the body of a crippled human so that he could be humbled and learn to respect the people of Midgard. Instead they opted to ignore this whole dichotomy. Maybe they felt it wouldn't make sense for aliens to be able to have that type of ability, but why make them aliens in the first place?

Another major flaw in this film is the awful romance between Thor and Jane Foster. Somehow Thor learns to love Jane, allowing him to sympathize with humanity, causing him to be able to wield Mjolnir again. In turn Jane somehow falls in love with Thor with no reasonable explanation. My guess is that it's because he's so darn handsome. It is simply a contrived loved story and the audience just has to buy into their love for one another. It would have made more sense if Jane Foster was in love with Donald Blake, like in the comics. There's also a terrible scene in which Odin is arguing with Loki and when things get really tense, he takes a nap. It's so awful and anti-climactic that it makes me cringe. In the end we have a film that established Thor as a really powerful alien and S.H.I.E.L.D. has firsthand knowledge of him. Tom Hiddleston's Loki is a bright spot but he wouldn't really shine on until later films.

Captain America (Yup, One More Time)

 **JASON**

With *Captain America: The First Avenger* (2011) we finally have a Steve Rogers America deserves! Building on the highly successful Marvel Studio formula, audiences were treated to a superb rendition of Captain America's origin. Using movie magic that can only be captured with modern technology, we go on a fantastic journey with Chris Evans starting as a sickly and weak boy and becoming the best Captain America put on screen. The first act of *Captain America: The First Avenger* is easily one of my favorite origin stories that I've seen.

The message of keeping true to your nature is powerful in this film and Chris Evans encapsulates the ideology so tremendously. After the first act however there are problems. Even though the struggle against Red Skull (played by villain for hire Hugo Weaving) is true to the comics it was unfortunate that they made him Hydra and not a Nazi. Obviously Marvel wanted to build up Hydra as the penultimate evildoers in the universe, but downplaying the struggle against the Nazis, I feel, is a disservice to the mythology of Captain America. When Bucky falls off a train in the film's third act is when this film loses its footing.

While the first part of the film was true to the mythos, the last part is just so poorly done that it keeps this film from being a true classic. I'll never understand why they didn't stick to the origin, in which both Bucky and Captain America's demise came at the hands of an explosion on a plane. It left a bitter taste in my mouth and prevents me from touting this as a comic book film classic. All of that aside this set up Captain America within the Marvel Cinematic Universe for future stories. It is yet another great example of how Marvel could tell a story while setting up future plots.

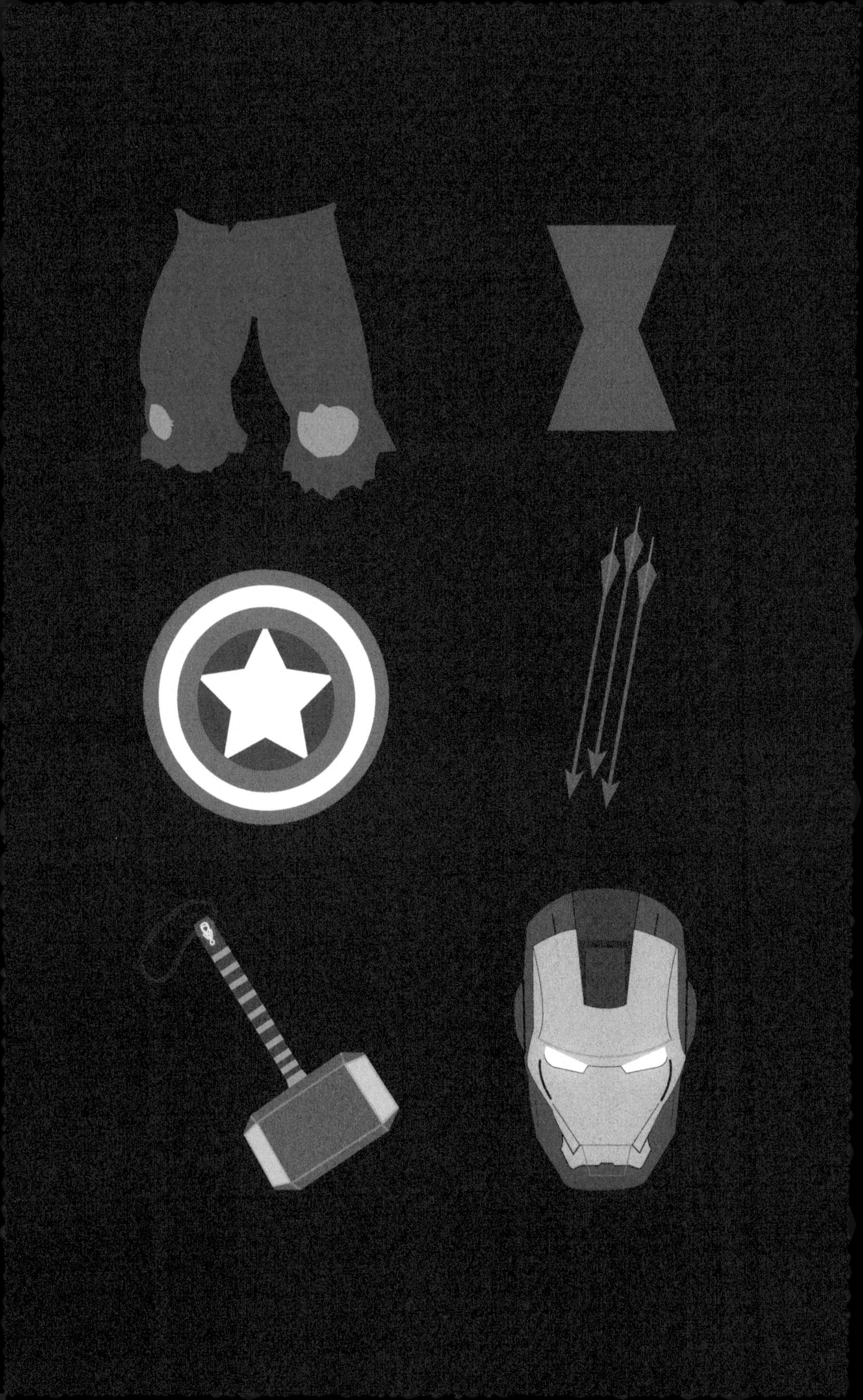

THE WINNING FORMULA (THE AVENGERS)

 **JASON**

If *Nick Fury: Agent of Shield* is the lowest point, then Joss Whedon's *The Avengers* is the highest point. It's hard to believe that this film came together the way it did. It can only be described as a comic book fanboy's dream come true. Its success rests mostly on the shoulders of the creative franchise assembling approach that Marvel Studios pioneered since *Iron Man*. When I first saw the film I was so very critical of it. Given the misgivings I had with films leading into this, such that *The Incredible Hulk* and *Thor* were not the films I had hoped for, all I did was look for flaws in *The Avengers*.

Upon a multiple viewings I couldn't help but fall in love with this film. I find it to be a filmmaking testament to how all comic book films should be approached. Who but Joss Whedon, a comic book lover and comic book writer, would be better to handle this film? Whedon has a way of getting people to seamlessly work together, somehow overcoming their character flaws to come together in the end for a common purpose. This of course is shown in the spectacular third act of the film, in which the audience is treated to a superhero extravaganza; one that has yet to be topped! There are so many gleeful superhero moments in this film that it's easy to overlook the subtle moments, such as with the Hulk and Black Widow that make this film memorable.

The biggest takeaway from this film is how Marvel Studios has created their own mythology from the films and not on the strength of the comic books they are derived from. We are now living in the world of the Marvel Cinematic Universe, which is separate from the Marvel Comic Book Universe. It is an extraordinary feat that might not be matched by other comic book franchises. This film is also notable because of the strength of Tom Hiddleston's Loki, the strongest of all the villains portrayed in the MCU. Villains in the MCU can be very black and white evil, but there is a depth to Hiddleston's performance and the writing of the character that make him very compelling. Could this be the cresting wave in comic book cinema? Perhaps. So let this film take you on a journey, and enjoy every minute of it.

 **BENNY**

Everything was set up for this film; it was supposed to be the big payoff for all of the Easter eggs set up in the series of movies leading up to it. With the success of every one of the previous films, it was assumed this one would be a success as well. But even Marvel couldn't have expected the response to the film. At the time of release, the movie became the third highest grossing film of all time, and even now as I write this it has maintained the fifth highest grossing film of all time— that's a higher spot than its own sequel.

That is technically where this story ends. *The Avengers* was the movie that cemented the years of superhero movies to come. It was 12 years in the making, becoming the first true superhero team-up film with modern day filming, excellent casting, and a budget that would do it justice. Everything is attempting to follow this model now. DC has announced its

Justice League universe and is using *Man of Steel* as its starter for this universe. FOX is taking their X-Men properties and trying to build a similar shared universe by introducing us to Deadpool and creating solo Wolverine films.

But now I want to allow my co-writers to speak their minds on the Marvel movies. Like we said at the start, we are just your average guys who enjoy comic books and movies. So what did a comic book storeowner and a comic newcomer to comic books think of it?

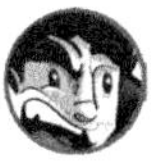

DAN

Finally, after all the individual superhero films, we got the all-star team-up with the release of Marvel's *The Avengers* in 2012. With the big heroes including Iron Man, Captain America, Thor, Hulk, and many others, the movie offered great effects, great fights, well-written dialogue, and great acting. However, that's not what made it great for me. What really made this film stand out was that it showed how different all superheroes really are from each other. In a movie that could have been overly complex given the number of characters and powers, I felt I was given clear insight into what was going on with each character, plus I could see their individual powers really in action. While the superheroes may have been given the same goal, each had very different ways of achieving that goal.

In *The Avengers*, it was great seeing that these people were far from perfect and had to put effort into working together as an actual team to defeat their enemies. Heroes still fight with each other (even to the point of starting their own civil war!), and I really enjoyed it because of that imperfection. It's easy to always picture superheroes as almost flawless but when they are put side-by-side and begin to open each other's eyes to their personal beliefs and methods for defeating evil, their humanity begins to show. Okay, maybe not so much for Thor, being a god and all, but you get my point.

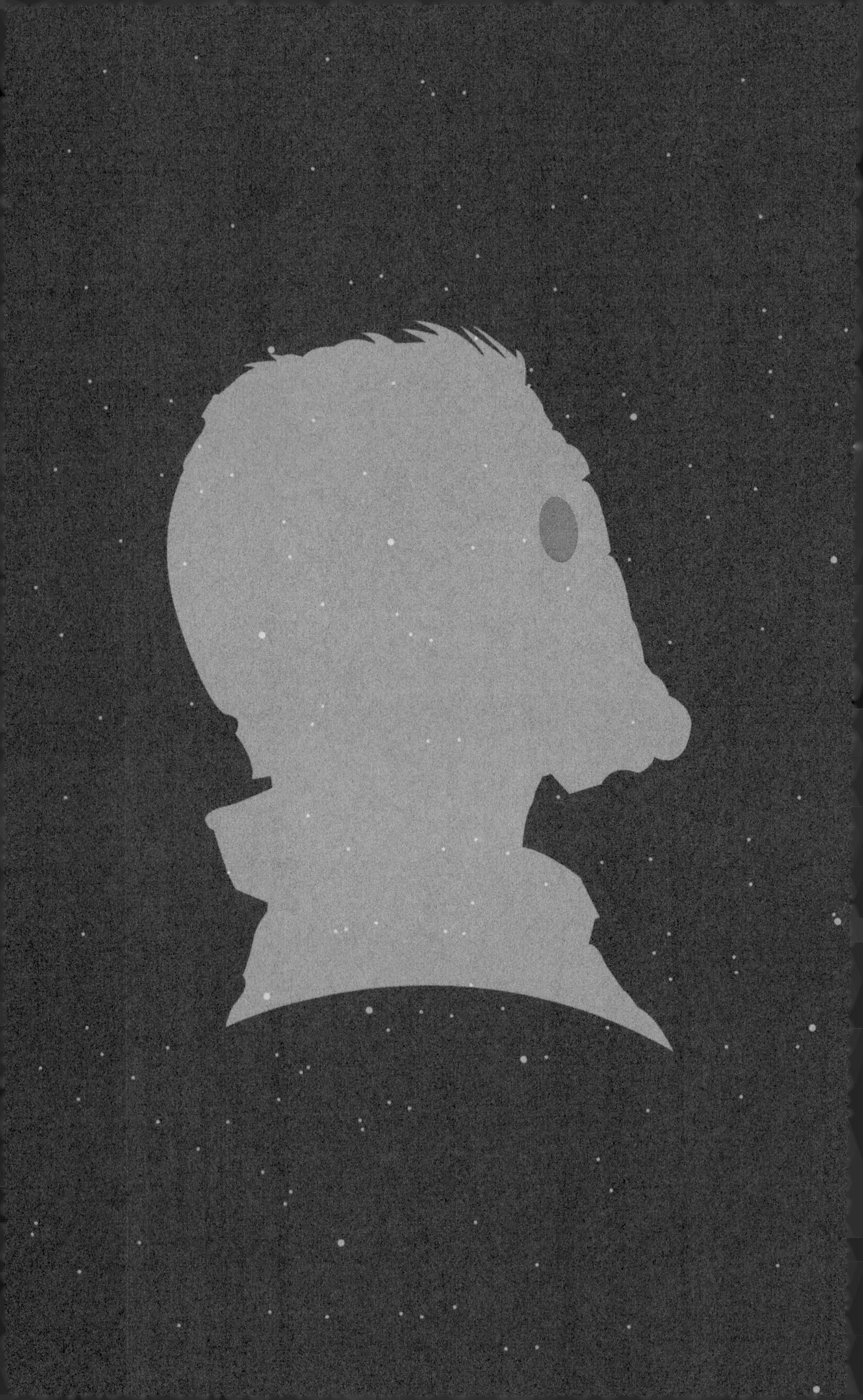

Guardians of the Galaxy

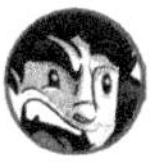 **DAN**

Two more Marvel movies I want to touch on are *Guardians of the Galaxy* (2014) and *Deadpool* (2016). *Guardians of the Galaxy* was a fantastic film; funny, exciting, adventurous, great music, and just a really solid movie. It's worth mentioning as part of Marvel's success because it showed that even the not-so popular heroes or teams can make a good movie. The Guardians weren't the most favored comic, but the film is a lot of people's favorite of all the Marvel movies released and it is obvious why when you watch it.

This is a tribute to the Marvel Cinematic Universe for stepping out of their comfort zone to create a movie based on, perhaps, a not-so-well known group that went on to became a phenomenal movie. Of course, this success, in turn, helped boost the comic. I know that I personally began reading the Guardian, Star-Lord, and The Rocket and Groot comics after seeing the movie. It showed that some characters, and stories, just belong on the big screen. Maybe we'll see more movies about other lesser-known superheroes.

Deadpool

Which brings us to Marvel's unconventional anti-hero, the merc with a mouth, Deadpool. Released in 2016, *Deadpool* showed that hero movies were not limited to saving the world but, instead for some characters, were all about personal vendettas that involve large amounts of dismemberment. *Deadpool* was so funny that it instantly joined my top three favorite comedy movies of all time. What made this movie great was how perfectly Ryan Reynolds portrayed Deadpool and how true to the comic book they kept the character. No punches were pulled in any of the violence, dialogue, or any part of the movie and that's what made it amazing—it was truly Deadpool.

This movie has opened up a potentially different and lucrative avenue for Marvel Studios. I felt like this was the first R rated Marvel movie to truly start to appeal to the adult crowd. While some may argue that *Blade* started this trend, I don't believe it did, as many viewers didn't view Blade as a superhero or part of Marvel. While *Blade* came across as a standard vampire hunter movie, we knew Deadpool was part of a hero world by the way he dressed and the fact that he talks and works with some of the X-Men. *Deadpool* has helped solidify Marvel's place on the big screen as it showed that there are a wide variety of Marvel movies, not just family friendly ones.

Starting out as terrible and moving on to be some of the most highly anticipated and highest earning movies of all time, Marvel has really found success. It's going to be exciting to see the continuation of the evolution of the Marvel franchise on the big screen. The Marvel Cinematic Universe has already shown itself to expand across the galaxy, so the possibilities are endless.

A FINAL LOOK BEHIND THE UNIVERSE

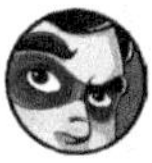

BENNY

The tale of Marvel is very different from the franchises of Superman and Batman. While Superman and Batman are very dividing due to the nature of the superheroes, Marvel is very inviting. This is, as I stated earlier, due to Batman and Superman being over 75 years old and so recognizable. No matter how Batman and Superman are handled, someone will dislike their representation. But when it comes to Marvel, while they are popular and have had some amazing comics before the movies, they weren't worldwide recognizable like DC's titans. This gave Marvel a major advantage because they could take their licenses, introduce characters like Iron Man, and only irritate the 100,000 comic purchases that month.

One fact people fail to realize is that comic book sales aren't in the millions. Successful comics sell around 20,000 copies and blockbusters only sell 150,000 to 200,000. While this may seem like a lot of fans, the fact of the matter is Marvel isn't dividing their fans because the heroes they are using aren't that well-known. The biggest problem Marvel had in their marketing push for *Iron Man* was trying to convince the public that Iron Man wasn't a robot, but a man in a suit. That right there tells you that Iron Man wasn't well known. This meant that people could go into Iron Man with zero expectations and just enjoy the film for what it was. Don't get me wrong, the Marvel movies found a formula that works and it's amazing. I am in love with each and every movie in their franchise.

But it's easier to get the masses on board when you can love the movie for what it is and not hate it for its portrayal of the hero.

While Batman and Superman divide their audiences more times than anyone can count, the Marvel movies are universally praised for what they have accomplished.

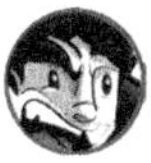

DAN

Marvel movies have had quite the journey to get to where they are now. Over the years, there were a lot of Marvel movies before Marvel found their movie mojo, starting with the very first Captain America movies in the 1940s. This Captain America was actually a serial but showed that movie companies at the time didn't really care about what they were supposed to do or how faithful they were to the comics, choosing to just run with the name and take it in any direction they wanted. This approach gave us a District Attorney Captain America with a pistol instead of a shield, maybe not the best start for Marvel movies on the big screen.

Marvel went on to make some more questionable adaptations, including a Spider-Man TV movie, *The Incredible Hulk* TV series, and *Howard the Duck*. This approach continued until 146

we got a second Captain America in 1990, which only further proved that movie companies really didn't know how to make superhero movies and maybe wouldn't ever deliver a success. In this Captain America film we had a slightly more accurate interpretation of the hero in terms of having a shield and working with the military, but that was about as far as its success went. Captain America was completely miscast, the Red Skull had the wrong accent, the shield throws quite literally turned Cap's shield into a boomerang, and there were even a couple of times that Captain America tricked people and stole their cars. Huh? Long story short, this film made it hard to believe that a good Marvel movie would ever come to fruition.

 **JASON**

The story of Marvel Studios is an incredible rise to power. Humble beginnings ending in a dominating performance, there seems to be no rival for what they put on the screen as far as comic books are concerned. I have to say that perhaps the ends have justified the anguish of suffering through so many failed comic book films. Usually going into these films I brace for the worst, holding onto my fond memories of the comic books. The nature of the stories are always presented faithfully while they might not be true to their source material in the way I would like these films to be. The journey is not over for Marvel Studios and thankfully it won't be for years to come. Rest assured when the Marvel logo appears at the beginning of a film viewers can expect quality entertainment, and in the end that is all I have ever wanted from these films.

FROM THE PAGES TO THE BIG SCREEN

 **BENNY**

Where do we go from here? It's been a journey that has seen its fair share of peaks and valleys (and peaks again). Will the genre remain on top? Critics, fans, geeks, and trolls behind Reddit threads will have their opinions. But I'm more interested in yours.

While the assumption is that the ever-growing fan base for superhero movies will eventually get tired of seeing the same thing over and over, companies like Marvel are already taking strides to mix up the formula. They are making movies that many expect will (and by this time, have) push the boundaries of characters, relationships and what we think we know about comics.

One movie we didn't get a chance to talk about—and currently remains one of my personal top two superhero films—is *Ant-Man*. This movie took the idea of a superhero flick and turned it into a heist movie with a superhero in it. It is ideas like this that will keep the superhero genre fresh for years to come.

There is also the culture of our world now: *geekdoms* are accepted. Comic-con is one of the hottest tickets around. This might also help comic book movies stay relevant and well-funded. If I can enjoy Batman comic books for 20 years, why couldn't I enjoy Batman movies for 20 years? If someone jumped on board with the Marvel movies when they were 10, why couldn't they remain a fan if the stories and cinematography remain as good as they are 20 years from now? Hopefully I'll have to write a sequel to this book in 10 years, discussing the DC Extended Universe and Marvels Phase 2 and 3 more in-depth. But until we get there, thank you to everyone who bought and read this book.

Until next time, true believers, excelsior.

AUTHOR BIOS

Benny Potter, a professional man-child, is the Comicstorian. With over 80 million views on YouTube, Potter (with the help of his team) has become the definitive source for all thing comic books online. As the executive producer for multiple YouTube channels, Potter has built up an audience with his unique brand of dramatic recaps on comic books, video games and movies. While managing multiple channels he also runs a YouTube mentorship program and has been producing content for other outlets. Potter spent 9 years in the military in multiple capacities and it was during this time that he developed his unique brand of teaching through entertainment. Whenever he has a moment to himself he likes to unwind by working on his personal comic series.

Jason Keen is the world's oldest teenager. He graduated from Colorado State University with a B.A. in History Education in 2004. Soon after he began to teach at the PIONEER School for Expeditionary Learning from 2004-2007, focusing on social studies. After leaving PIONEER he began working at Grand Slam Sports Cards and Comics in Loveland, Colorado with his older brother Kevin where to this day they continue to sells sports cards, comics, games, and toys. The self-proclaimed "analog" gamer, Keen is also an accomplished musician releasing his album Freedom Fries in 2004. He started writing and contributing for the YouTuber Comicstorian 2014. He lives in Ft. Collins, Colorado with his mother and brother and has no plans for growing up anytime soon.

Dan Rumbles has been the editor for the Comicstorian YouTube channel since the beginning of 2015. Prior to this role, Rumbles was a coffee aficionado. He has made videos that have aired on countless channels across the Internet including the DC YouTube channel. In his free time he enjoys reading comics, riding his motorcycle, playing video games, and being the super cool guy that he is.

CPSIA information can be obtained at www.ICGtesting.com
Printed in the USA
BVOW05s1514150816

458371BV00015B/12/P

9 781633 533431